BOOK OF THE
HORSE

SUSAN McBANE &
HELEN DOUGLAS-COOPER

SELECT
EDITIONS

A QUINTET BOOK

Copyright© 1995 Quintet Publishing Limited.
This book may not be reproduced in whole or in part, in any
means, electronic or mechanical, including photocopying,
recording or by any information storage and or retrieval system
now known or hereafter invented, without written permission
from the publisher and copyright holder.

ISBN: 1-85348-908-5

This book was designed and produced by
Quintet Publishing Limited

Consultant Editor: Pamela MacGregor-Morris
Technical Consultant: Jane Starkey
Editorial Director: Jeremy Harwood
Art Director: Alastair Campbell
Art Editor: David Mallott
Editors: Jenny Barling, Marion Casey,
Alastair Dougall, David MacFadyen
Designer: Marnie Searchwell
Illustrators: Kai Choi, Harry Clow, Christopher Forsey,
Tony Graham, Rory Kee, Elaine Keenan, Edwina Keene,
Abdul Aziz Khan, Kathleen McDougall, John Woodcock,
Clive Haybal, Martin Woodford, Kathy Wyatt, Jim Marks
Photographers: Mike Busselle, Mike Fear,
Colin Maher, Jay Swallow, Jon Wyand
Picture Research: Maggie Colbeck, Linda Proud
Jacket Design: Louise Morley, Nik Morley

Typeset in Great Britain by
Vantage Photosetting Co. Ltd

Produced in Australia by Griffin Colour

Published by Selectabook Limited,
Devizes.

Contents

The points of the horse

The most striking feature of the horse is that it can perform the many tasks asked of it by man, though its physical make-up is in many ways unsuited to such demands. In its main period of evolution, the horse developed from a four or even five-toed marsh dweller to take the basic form it has today at a relatively early date; and even though it has somewhat changed its shape and improved its performance, the basic working mechanism remains the same.

Such basic physical facts should always colour the rider's attitude to the horse, and what he or she expects of it. With a basic understanding of the so-called points of the horse, it should be possible, for example, to go some way towards lessening the risk of muscular strains. These are all too common and, in extreme cases, can lead to a horse having to rest for weeks, if not months. More important still, knowledge of these points acts as a valuable guide in deciding what is a suitable or unsuitable horse for the prospective rider. The most vital attribute of any riding horse is depth of girth, which denotes toughness and strength. Tall, leggy horses invariably lack stamina. Short legs and a deep body, with plenty of heart room, are the signs to look for.

The most important points of the horse are its limbs and feet. Both in the wild and in domesticity, the horse depends on its means of locomotion for survival.

Feet and legs require therefore to be as correctly conformed as possible, if the horse is to remain sound and mobile. Correct conformation is, indeed, the most valuable asset any horse can possess.

The hind leg
Experts differ as to whether the most important single asset is a good hind leg or a good foreleg. As the hind leg is the propelling force, it is usually given priority. At the point

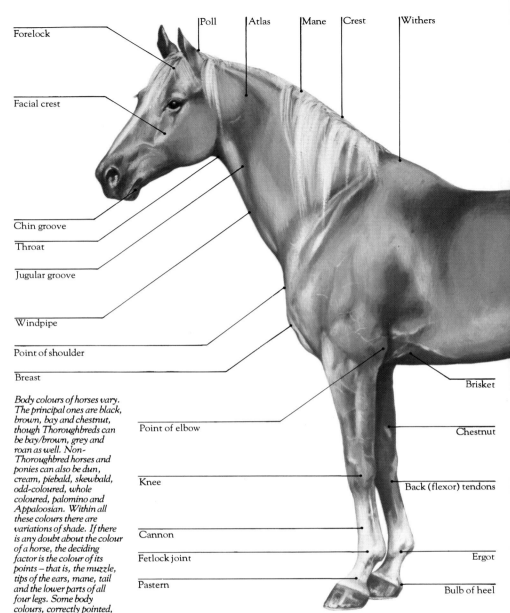

Body colours of horses vary. The principal ones are black, brown, bay and chestnut, though Thoroughbreds can be bay/brown, grey and roan as well. Non-Thoroughbred horses and ponies can also be dun, cream, piebald, skewbald, odd-coloured, whole coloured, palomino and Appaloosian. Within all these colours there are variations of shade. If there is any doubt about the colour of a horse, the deciding factor is the colour of its points — that is, the muzzle, tips of the ears, mane, tail and the lower parts of all four legs. Some body colours, correctly pointed, are shown (below).

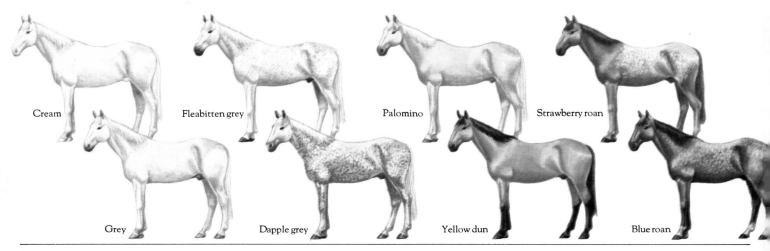

Cream

Grey

Fleabitten grey

Dapple grey

Palomino

Yellow dun

Strawberry roan

Blue roan

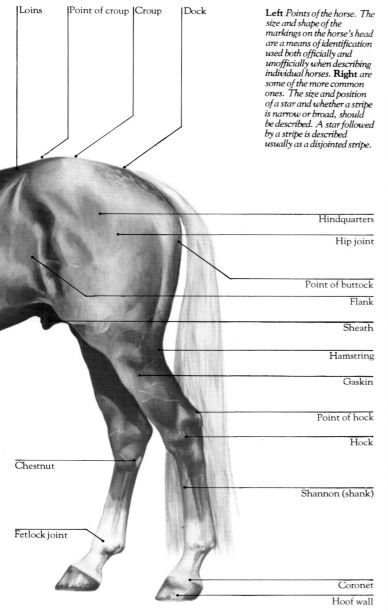

Loins | Point of croup | Croup | Dock

Hindquarters

Hip joint

Point of buttock

Flank

Sheath

Hamstring

Gaskin

Point of hock

Hock

Chestnut

Shannon (shank)

Fetlock joint

Coronet

Hoof wall

Left *Points of the horse. The size and shape of the markings on the horse's head are a means of identification used both officially and unofficially when describing individual horses.* **Right** *are some of the more common ones. The size and position of a star and whether a stripe is narrow or broad, should be described. A star followed by a stripe is described usually as a disjointed stripe.*

White face

Stripe

Blaze

Snip

Star

Right *White leg markings are an important means of identification. A sock covers the fetlock and part of the cannon, while a stocking extends to the knee or hock. Other marks take the name of their site.*

Chestnut

Bay

Piebald

Odd coloured

Liver chestnut

Brown

Skewbald

Black

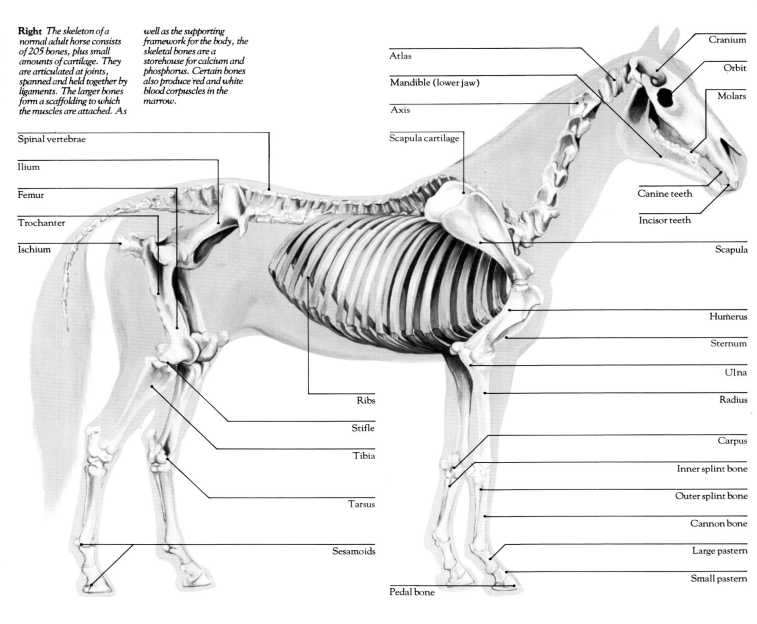

Right *The skeleton of a normal adult horse consists of 205 bones, plus small amounts of cartilage. They are articulated at joints, spanned and held together by ligaments. The larger bones form a scaffolding to which the muscles are attached. As well as the supporting framework for the body, the skeletal bones are a storehouse for calcium and phosphorus. Certain bones also produce red and white blood corpuscles in the marrow.*

Spinal vertebrae

Ilium

Femur

Trochanter

Ischium

Atlas

Mandible (lower jaw)

Axis

Scapula cartilage

Cranium

Orbit

Molars

Canine teeth

Incisor teeth

Scapula

Humerus

Sternum

Ulna

Radius

Carpus

Inner splint bone

Outer splint bone

Cannon bone

Large pastern

Small pastern

Ribs

Stifle

Tibia

Tarsus

Sesamoids

Pedal bone

Left *Three consecutive stages of the gallop are shown in a skeletal diagram. The moment of suspension, with all four feet off the ground, reveals how the hindlegs are gathered in through the action of the hock and stifle joints, which are the main propelling force.*

Below Left *Three phases of a jump – take off, flight and landing – show hock and stifle joints in action again, powering the spring and gathering up the hindlegs to clear the obstacle. The unique structure of the foreleg, which is attached to the upper body solely by muscles and ligaments, cushions the spine from the concussive shock of the landing.*

Far Left *This view of the horse's skeleton from the front shows the thoracic inlet – the bony ring through which the trachea and oesophagus enter the chest cavity. From the rear (**Left**) the pelvic bones are shown.*

able ride, they, too, are a sign of weakness that could lead to future trouble.

The foot

The size of foot varies with the type of horse. Thoroughbreds usually have small, rounded feet and, often, low heels. Heavy breeds, such as Clydesdales, Shires and Percherons, have larger, flatter feet.

The foot should be wide and open, not narrow, 'boxy' and contracted. The horn should look healthy and be free from unsightly cracks or ridges. Under it lies the sensitive laminae.

When the foot is lifted up, a well-developed frog should be visible on the underside. Starting at the bulbs of the heel and running upwards to end in a point near the toe, the frog acts as an anti-slip device and also helps to absorb concussion.

Each hoof is surmounted by the coronary band, which lies between the foot and the pastern.

Proper care of the feet is vital. In jumping, for instance, one forefoot has to take the whole weight of both horse and rider at the moment of landing. Good shoeing is therefore essential, or lameness will result. A young horse, too, can develop a form of lameness called pedal ostitis, caused by an excess of pressure on the sensitive sole of the foot by the os pedis – the terminal bone. This comes about largely through overwork, particularly in jumping.

The foreleg

The unique feature of the horse's foreleg is that it is attached to the upper part of the body by nothing more than muscle and ligamentous tissue. The horse has no equivalent to the human clavicle, or collar bone. The chief advantage of this is that the muscle is able to absorb a great deal of the concussion that would otherwise be transmitted to the spine. However, if undue strain is placed on the muscle, the horse can easily break down. This is particularly the case in race horses – often because the horse is what is known as 'back at the knee' (the shape is concave rather than convex).

The foreleg extends from the body below the point of the shoulder. The forearm runs down into the knee, which, like the hock, should be big, flat and prominent. Then the cannon bone, with tendons standing out clear and hard, runs down into the fetlock. The pastern separates this from the foot.

The legs have one final individual feature – the horny growths inside the legs above the knees. These are called chestnuts, and are, like fingerprints, completely individual. They are thought to be the remains of a digit.

where it emerges from the body the stifle joint is situated. This corresponds to the human knee and is similarly equipped with a patella, or kneecap. This acts like a pulley block to give added strength to the muscles extending the stifle.

The stifle itself is synchronized in its movements with the hock, as it is controlled by the same muscles and ligaments. As one flexes, so does the other.

Then comes the gaskin, or second thigh. This should be muscular and well-developed enough to stand up to the work and strain demanded of it. This runs down into the hock – probably the most important part of the leg as the main propelling agent which enables the horse to gallop and jump.

The hock is made up of a whole series of joints, tightly bound together by ligaments. It articulates directly with the tibia (another

vital bone) only through one bone – the astralagus. The feature as a whole should be big, flat and free from unsightly lumps, bumps or swellings. These can be indications of various types of unsoundness, such as curbs, spavins or thoroughpins.

The hock should also be near to the ground; short cannon bones from hock to fetlock and from knee to fetlock are a sign of strength. The tendons should stand out sharply and there should be no thickening of the lower leg.

The fetlock joint should also be well-defined and not puffy – a puffy fetlock resembles a human swollen ankle. This leads on to the pastern, which should be of medium length and slope. Very short pasterns cannot fulfill one of their main tasks – absorbing the concussion produced by movement. Though over-long pasterns give a springy, comfort-

The body

The shoulder runs from the withers – the bony prominence dividing the neck from the back and the highest part of the dorsal spine – down to the point of the shoulder. The shoulder itself should be long and sloping, especially at the upper end. An upright shoulder reduces endurance, as the horse has to do more work to cover the ground, and it cannot help to reduce concussion, which instead is passed on to the rider, making the horse uncomfortable to ride. This is particularly the case if the horse is ridden downhill.

The breast lies to the front of the shoulder, between the forelegs. It should be broad and muscular; narrow-breasted horses are weak and lack stamina. The underside of the neck should be concave and not unduly muscular.

The jaws run down to the muzzle. Well-defined, slightly distended nostrils and a

large, generous eye are a sign of quality and good breeding. So are alert, well-pricked ears, which should not be too large. Between them lies the poll, leading to the top of neck, the crest, which runs down to the withers and back. The back consists of about eleven of the eighteen dorsal vertebrae, as well as the arches of the corresponding ribs. Behind it lie the loins, which should be strong and well-muscled. These extend to the croup, or rump, which runs down to the tail and its underside, the dock.

Standing behind the horse, the points of the hip can be seen projecting outwards on either side of the backbone, above the flanks. This outwards projection means that they can easily be injured.

Just below the loins, a triangular depression, known as the 'hollow of the flank', is located. This is the highest point of the

flank, which stretches downwards from the lumbar spine. The condition of the flank often acts as a guide to the health of the horse; if the horse is sick, it may well be 'tucked up' or distended.

Teeth and age

Age in the horse is determined by examining the six incisors (grinding teeth). The two central incisors are cut when a foal is ten days old and are followed within a month or six weeks by the lateral incisors. The corner incisors follow between six and nine months, to complete the horse's full set of milk teeth.

The trot (below) is an active, two-time pace, the legs moving in diagonal pairs with a moment of suspension. The rider rises in the saddle for one stride, then sits again.

The walk (right) is the slowest pace of the horse. The animal moves one leg after another in the sequence, left fore, right hind, right fore, left hind, in a regular four-time rhythm.

Trot

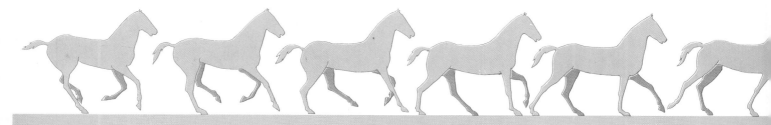

Canter

Gallop

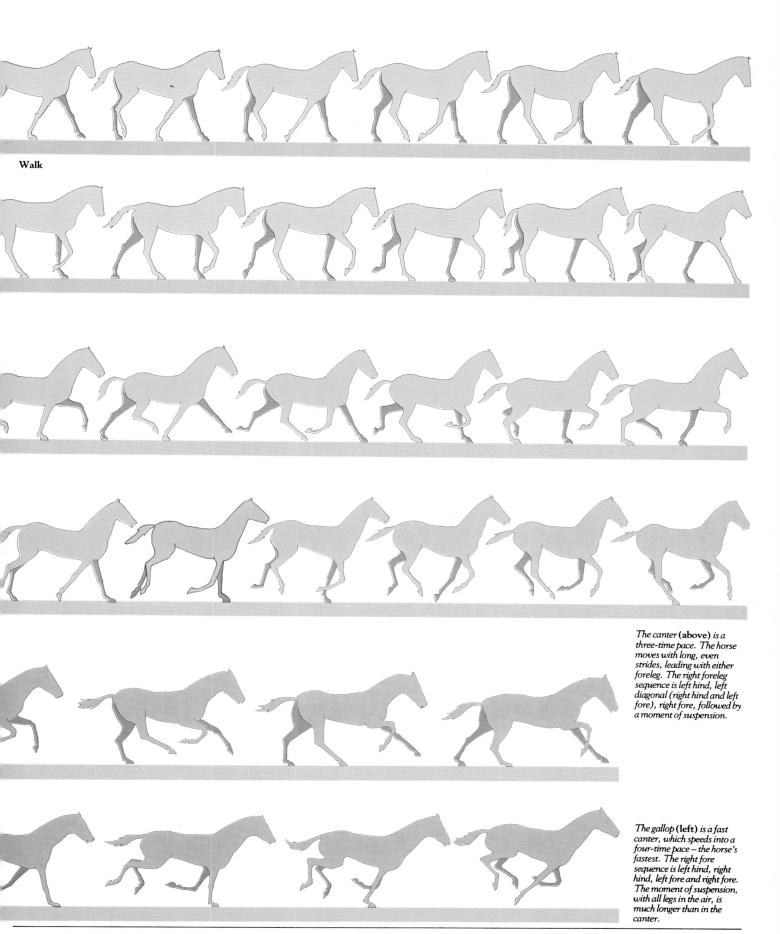

Walk

The canter (**above**) is a
three-time pace. The horse
moves with long, even
strides, leading with either
foreleg. The right foreleg
sequence is left hind, left
diagonal (right hind and left
fore), right fore, followed by
a moment of suspension.

The gallop (**left**) is a fast
canter, which speeds into a
four-time pace – the horse's
fastest. The right fore
sequence is left hind, right
hind, left fore and right fore.
The moment of suspension,
with all legs in the air, is
much longer than in the
canter.

Basic riding

The key to learning to ride is basically one of confidence. The rider must have faith in his or her ability to communicate with, control and work with the horse; equally, the horse must have confidence in its rider. The only way to achieve this is to find a good instructor, who has the knack of encouraging his or her pupils to approach their lessons in a calm and relaxed manner. Riding is supposed to be a pleasure, so do not go to a hectoring instructor or trainer, who may turn this wonderful sport into a weekly nightmare.

The search can be a bewildering one, as level, competence and type of instruction often varies. Approval by a recognized riding association is always a sign of quality. In the UK, the British Horse Society (BHS) and the Association of British Riding Schools both publish lists of stables that have been inspected and approved; in the USA, the American Horse Shows Association does the same. In Australia, though there is no national system of assessment as such, the magazine *Australian Horse and Rider* publishes similar surveys.

The clothes to wear

At first there is no need to spend money on a full riding kit, but certain items are essential for both safety and comfort. A hard riding hat, or, better still, a racing-style crash helmet, is one of them, but make sure that the brand you buy meets national safety requirements. Jodhpur boots, western riding boots, or rubber riding boots (these are far cheaper than leather ones) are also vital. Plimsolls can slip through the stirrup irons and rubber wellingtons are not really the right shape.

Otherwise clothes can be adapted to purse and needs. A thick, close-fitting pair of jeans (not the 'flared' variety), or a pair of 'chaps', worn cowboy-style over a pair of trousers, can take the place of breeches or jodhpurs at first. These should be worn with a thick sweater or windcheater in winter, or, in hot weather, a tee-shirt or sports shirt. A riding mackintosh is a good investment, as is a pair of string gloves. Wet reins, especially if also slippery with sweat, can be almost impossible to grip.

Handling, mounting and dismounting

At first, the horse should be 'made ready' for you, but it is a good idea to ask if you can bring your mount out of its box and into the yard to get used to being around such a big animal. Greet the horse calmly and move to its shoulder, talking to it as you do so. Then, run your hand down the shoulder and give it a pat. Move to its head, undo the head-collar and lead the horse out of the box.

The next stage is to mount the horse – either unaided, or assisted by a leg-up. Begin-

The principles of classical riding were laid down by a sixteenth century Neapolitan riding master Federico Grisone in 1550. In them, the horseman used a straight leg and fixed-hand reins controlling the horse with a powerful curb bit and spurs. The rider dominated the horse completely, forcing it into intricate dressage movements. Grisone's influence was widespread and long-lasting, particularly in the various high schools of the royal courts of Europe. A present day survival is the Spanish School in Vienna and its famous Lipizzaner horses (left).

With the dawn of the twentieth century came a revolution in riding which transformed the art of equitation. This was the creation of the Forward Seat by an Italian cavalry officer, Federico Caprilli (1867–1907). His system was based on a partnership between horse and rider, the aim being to interfere with the horse as little as possible and so allow it to move freely and with natural balance.

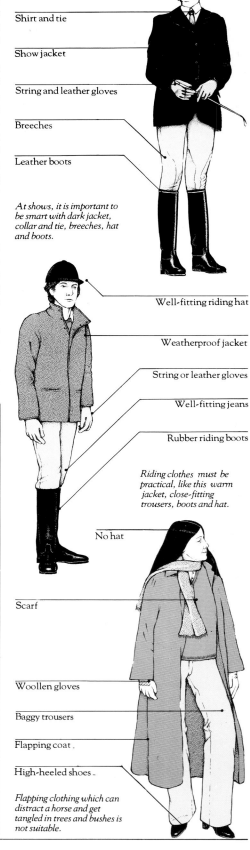

Riding hat
Shirt and tie
Show jacket
String and leather gloves
Breeches
Leather boots

At shows, it is important to be smart with dark jacket, collar and tie, breeches, hat and boots.

Well-fitting riding hat
Weatherproof jacket
String or leather gloves
Well-fitting jeans
Rubber riding boots

Riding clothes must be practical, like this warm jacket, close-fitting trousers, boots and hat.

No hat
Scarf
Woollen gloves
Baggy trousers
Flapping coat
High-heeled shoes

Flapping clothing which can distract a horse and get tangled in trees and bushes is not suitable.

Holding the headpiece in the left hand, put the reins over the horse's head and neck first. The horse will then be under control while the headpiece is being fitted. Make sure that no part of the bridle trails on the ground.

Hold the headpiece up in the right hand and cradle the bit on the thumb and forefinger of the left. Then slip the left hand under the horse's muzzle and insert a finger between its front and back teeth on the offside to open the mouth.

Having slipped the bit into the mouth, use both hands to bring the headpiece over its ears, one at a time. Smooth the forelock down over the browband and check that this is clear of the ears. See that no part of the headpiece is twisted.

Then fasten the throatlash and nose band. There should be a hand's width between throatlash and jaw and noseband. See that the bit is not low enough to rest on the teeth, or high enough to wrinkle the horse's lips.

With the horse tied up, smooth the saddle area of the coat before picking up the saddle by its front arch and cantle, and placing it lightly but firmly on the horse's withers. Then slide it back enough to let the horse's shoulders move freely.

Check that all is smooth under saddle flap, then move to the offside and let down girth, which has been lying over saddle. Return to nearside and buckle the girth firmly, so that a hand can just be slipped beneath it. Saddling can be done in one operation.

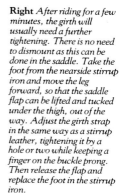

Right *After riding for a few minutes, the girth will usually need a further tightening. There is no need to dismount as this can be done in the saddle. Take the foot from the nearside stirrup iron and move the leg forward, so that the saddle flap can be lifted and tucked under the thigh, out of the way. Adjust the girth strap in the same way as a stirrup leather, tightening it by a hole or two while keeping a finger on the buckle prong. Then release the flap and replace the foot in the stirrup iron.*

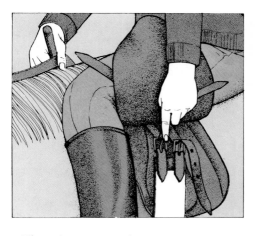

ners should always have a groom standing at the horse's head to ensure that the animal stands still while being mounted.

Always mount a horse from the near (left) side. Before doing so, check the girth for tightness; if it is too loose, the saddle may slip as the rider's weight comes on to the stirrup. Gather the reins in the left hand, maintaining a light contact with the horse's mouth. Take care not to keep the left rein too short, or the horse may start to circle as you mount.

Place the left hand on the pommel of the saddle and then turn the body so that your back is to the horse's head with the left shoulder parallel with the horse's left shoulder. Take the left stirrup iron with the right hand, turn it clockwise towards you and place the ball of the left foot in the iron, keeping the toe as low as possible. If it digs into the horse's flank, it will act as a signal to the horse to move forward.

Place the right hand over the waist of the saddle, and, with the weight of the body on the left foot, spring upwards from the right foot, using the right hand as a lever. Bring the right leg over the saddle and then gently lower yourself into it. Place the right foot in the offside iron and take up the reins with both hands.

To dismount, take both feet out of the irons and collect the reins in one hand.

Then, swinging the right leg well over the cantle of the saddle, gently, but briskly, vault off, landing on both feet.

Adjusting the stirrups

Once in the saddle, the next thing to do is tighten the girth again and then adjust the stirrup leathers to the correct length. The initial temptation at the start of a ride is to have the leathers too short. As the ride progresses, and the seat comes properly down into the saddle, it will be necessary to lengthen them.

To establish the correct length, take the feet out of the irons and let them hang down naturally. The iron should just touch the inside point of the ankle bone. Adjust the leathers accordingly, making sure that they are both the same length.

The seat

The seat is the rock on which all good riding is founded; without a correct position in the saddle, no pupil can hope to go on to advanced equitation successfully. A correct seat means that the rider is in balance – secure, light, and responsive to the horse's every movement. It is used in rhythm with the animal's action; the pushing down of the seat bones on the horse's back encourages it to lengthen its stride.

The rider sits into the middle and lowest part of the saddle, the body position being upright and free from stiffness, especially round the waist. The rider is in fact sitting on a triangle, two points being the seat bones and the third the crotch of the body.

The back should be straight, but relaxed and supple, with the shoulders held square. The head should always be held up and looking to the front. Never look down, or the back will become rounded and the chest hollowed. As a guide, place a hand behind you flat on the saddle. There should be room for the flat hand between you and the cantle.

The temptation to grip with knees and calves must be avoided. Otherwise the body will be stiffened, the seat raised out of the saddle and the position made rigid. The thighs and legs should wrap around the horse and mould themselves to the correct position. A simple routine to help achieve this is to open the legs away from the horse's flanks and then draw the thighs into position from behind. This will bring the large inside-thigh muscle under and to the back of the thigh, flattening the area and allowing it to rest close to the saddle and the horse. Then, by pushing the weight down on the ankles, the rider will feel the seat lower into the saddle.

The lower leg should hang down to rest lightly against the horse's sides, just behind

When mounting place left hand on the saddle pommel and put ball of left foot into iron with right hand, keeping toe low.

Next place right hand over waist of saddle and, keeping the toe under the horse against the girth, spring smoothly and lightly up.

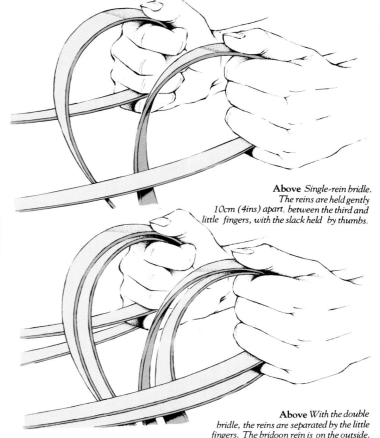

Above *Single-rein bridle. The reins are held gently 10cm (4ins) apart, between the third and little fingers, with the slack held by thumbs.*

Above *With the double bridle, the reins are separated by the little fingers. The bridoon rein is on the outside.*

Bring the right leg over, keeping it well clear of the saddle and the back of the horse. This should be done in one smooth movement.

Dismounting. First take both feet from the stirrup irons, transfer the reins to the left hand and grip pommel with the right hand.

Left *When mounted adjust stirrups by pulling the top leather up against the buckle under the saddle skirt. Keep a finger on the buckle spike – the leather can then be easily adjusted up or* *down.* **Below left** *The iron should hang level with the point of the ankle bone.* **Below right** *Secure top leather through keeper on saddle.*

Next, leaning forward lightly swing both legs clear of the horse, keeping weight on right hand and holding reins with the left.

Land lightly on both feet, facing the saddle and still keeping control with the reins in gentle contact with the horse's mouth.

the girth with the heel pressed down. This is where the rider's weight is balanced. Holding the lower leg too far forward or too far back must be avoided, because it affects the position in the saddle and makes it difficult to apply the leg aids correctly. Only the ball of the foot should rest in the stirrup iron, and both feet should be held parallel with the horse's sides.

If the position is correct, the rider's ears, shoulders, hips and heels should be in line with each other. The stirrup leather should be at right angles to the ground when the rider is mounted.

The arms should hang down naturally to the elbow. The hands, with thumbs uppermost, are held as if carrying two glasses of water. The rider should not get into the habit of bending the wrists inwards or of flattening the hand. A straight line should run from the elbow through the hand to the bit in the horse's mouth.

The best place to work on the correct saddle position is on the lunge rein, where most of the student's early work is usually done in any case. When working on the lunge, the rider should be holding a neckstrap, and not the reins. The horse is being controlled from the lunge; two people trying to direct it, one with the lunge and the other

from the bridle, will only confuse the animal.

A strong independent seat can only be achieved by regular active riding, assisted by suppling exercises and riding without stirrups. These are essential for developing balance and confidence.

The aids

The aids are the system of signals used to control the horse. They fall into two categories; first come the natural aids of hands, legs, seat and voice, and second are the artificial aids of whip, spurs, draw reins, drop nosebands, martingales and so on. The only one a beginner should use is a whip.

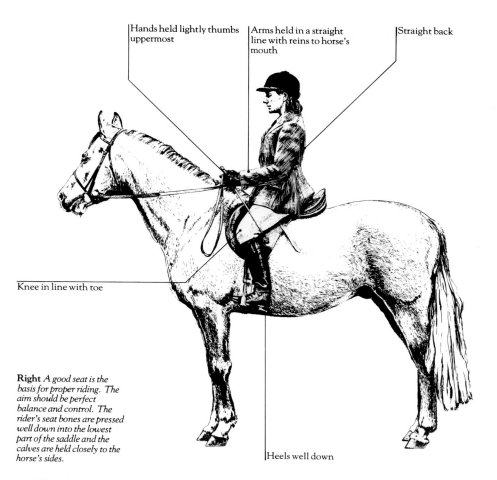

Hands held lightly thumbs uppermost

Arms held in a straight line with reins to horse's mouth

Straight back

Knee in line with toe

Heels well down

Right *A good seat is the basis for proper riding. The aim should be perfect balance and control. The rider's seat bones are pressed well down into the lowest part of the saddle and the calves are held closely to the horse's sides.*

All riding is based on controlling the natural impulsion of the horse. This is achieved by combined use of the rider's legs and seat. The aim is to get the horse moving freely and actively forward in the desired direction, and not evading the aids when they are applied. The rider can usually tell this through the hands; if the horse is resisting, there will be little 'feel' on the reins when activity is being asked for, and 'pull' if the horse is being checked.

The legs are used in a squeezing action just behind the girth. A quick, light squeeze, repeated if necessary, is more effective than prolonged pressure. Use of the heels should be avoided.

If the horse does not respond to the legs, the whip can be used to reinforce the aid. A tap on the horse's ribs, just behind the rider's leg, is usually adequate. Note that the whip is only an extension of the aid. It should not be used as a punishment except in extreme cases of disobedience.

Use of the hands

The hands control, never create, pace and direction through the use of the reins. Contact with the mouth should therefore be light and steady; pulling on the reins will only hurt and upset the horse. The wrists should be

supple and flexible enough to follow the horse's natural rhythm; the aim is to achieve a passive hand, not a rigid one with the wrists set in a fixed position.

It is essential therefore to hold the reins correctly. With a single-rein bridle, the reins should pass between the little finger and the third finger of each hand. The remainder of the reins pass through the finger and thumb, with the thumb on top of the rein to aid the grip. Double bridles, however, can be held in several different ways. One of them is to divide the reins with the little finger of each hand, with the curb (lower) rein crossing inside to pass between the third finger and little finger. Again, the reins pass out through the index finger and thumb, with the remainder crossing over to the left.

The walk

All early work should be done at the walk until the pupil has established the basic confidence required to move on to the other paces. Take up contact with the mouth and apply the aids to make the horse walk on. Keep the hands relaxed when the walk has been established, however, or the horse may be tempted to go into a trot.

Any unwanted increase in pace should be checked by closing the hands to resist the

forward movement, closing the legs to the sides and pushing down in the saddle with the seat bones. In response, the horse checks its pace. After a few strides, the rider should give with the hands, increase the pressure of the leg and seat aids and ask the horse to walk on again.

To ask for the halt, the rider applies both leg and seat pressure at the same time as lightly resisting the forward movement with the hands. The horse should stand still on all fours when it comes to the halt.

Changes of direction should also be learned and practised at the walk. The inside leg and hand ask for these, while the outside hand and leg control the pace. To go to the right, ask with the right hand, keeping the left one passive. Both legs should be closed to the horse to maintain the walk, but apply the left leg more strongly to prevent the swing of the quarters. To turn to the left, reverse the procedure.

The rider should make a conscious effort to think right or left. This concentration can act as a reinforcement to the physical aids being applied.

The trot

This is a two-time gait, in which the horse moves its legs in a diagonal sequence of near-fore, off-hind, off-fore and near-hind. Near-fore and off-hind make up what is known as the left diagonal; off-fore and near-hind the right. The rider can either sit in the saddle and follow the natural rhythm of the trot, or rise (post) slightly out of the saddle for one beat of the gait.

To achieve the transition from walk to trot, sit down in the saddle, close the legs and feel the inside rein. As the horse gets into its trot, sit into it for a few strides, using the legs to maintain the activity.

In the rising trot, the rider rises out of the saddle on one beat of one diagonal and descends on the other, with the weight of the body supported by the ankles, heels and stirrup irons, but not by the knees. These must act purely as a hinge. Rise from the hip, keeping the lower leg still. The thigh and body should remain at the same angle. Keep the horse moving forward and a light and even contact with the animal's mouth.

The seat should never be allowed to come completely out of the saddle and the reins should never be used as a lever when rising. In addition, always regularly change from one diagonal to the other. Like human beings, horses tend to favour one side of their body to the other, and this means that it is very easy to always remain on, say, the left diagonal during a prolonged period at the trot. This is bad for the horse as well as for the rider.

Right *The natural aids are the movements which communicate the rider's intentions to the horse. The body, legs and hands work together in complete harmony. If the horse is positioned and prepared correctly it can obey the rider's instructions more easily.*

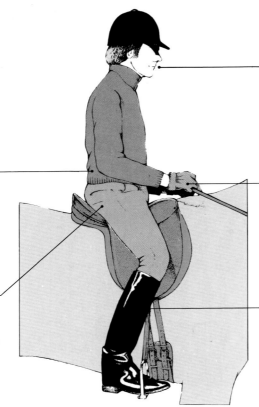

The voice can be used to soothe or check the horse.

The back muscles affect the seat. They make it more secure and enable the rider to maintain balance. Straightening the spine, combined with corresponding leg and hand actions conveys the rider's intentions to the horse.

The hands should be light and responsive, being used in a give-and-take action. They regulate the energy created by the calves, and control the forehand.

Pressure from the seat encourages the horse to move forward from the hindquarters. A firm, deep seat enables the rider to use the legs correctly.

The calves control impulsion and energy in the hindquarters and guide their direction.

lead the horse to increase the speed of its trot.

The horse should always lead off into the canter with the correct leg. The sequence always begins with a hind – off-hind if going to the left and near-hind to the right. The near-fore and off-fore are the two leading front legs respectively. A horse that starts to canter with the wrong lead is said to be cantering 'false'.

It is easier to establish the correct lead if the aids for the canter are applied on a bend, when the horse's body should be bent in the direction it is going. Thus, it usually balances itself naturally to take up the canter on the desired leg. The best way to establish a good canter, therefore, is to work in a large circle. The horse should maintain an active, rhyth-

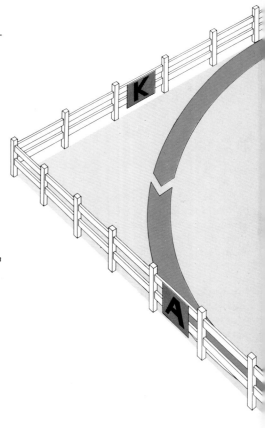

To change diagonals, simply sit down in the saddle for two beats, and then start rising again on the other diagonal, using the leg to give added impulsion if there is resistance. Diagonals should always be changed with each change of direction. For example, if trotting to the right on the left diagonal and then changing the rein to the left, the rider should shift his or her weight to the right diagonal. This keeps the horse level, balanced and gives it a 'breather'. In long distance riding, or hacking, the diagonal at the trot should be changed regularly.

To return to the walk, sit well down in the saddle, close the hands firmly and apply the leg aids until the horse walks forward freely. Give with the hands but keep applying the leg aids until the momentum of the walk is firmly established.

The canter

The canter is a three-time gait, with one beat coming from each of the forelegs and the third from the hindlegs. The rider relaxes with this rhythm, keeping a steady, even contact with the mouth. Sit deeply into the saddle, allowing the back to follow the movement from the hips, and avoid the temptation to be tipped forward. Over excitement – and kicking hard with the heels – will only

Left *Exercises strengthen the muscles and improve the rider's seat. They help the inexperienced rider gain confidence. The rider leans forward and down over the horse's neck to touch the left toe with the right hand. Then the rider sits upright and repeats the process on the other side.*

With arms outstretched outwards, head up and back straight the rider turns as far as possible in each direction, twisting the body from the hips. This improves the suppleness of the back and waist. This exercise can be practised at the halt or when the horse is moving at a walk.

With arms folded, the rider leans back to rest on the horse's quarters, then sits upright again. The legs should remain in the correct riding position during the exercise. Do not attempt this, or any other, exercise on an inexperienced horse which may be frightened by the movements involved.

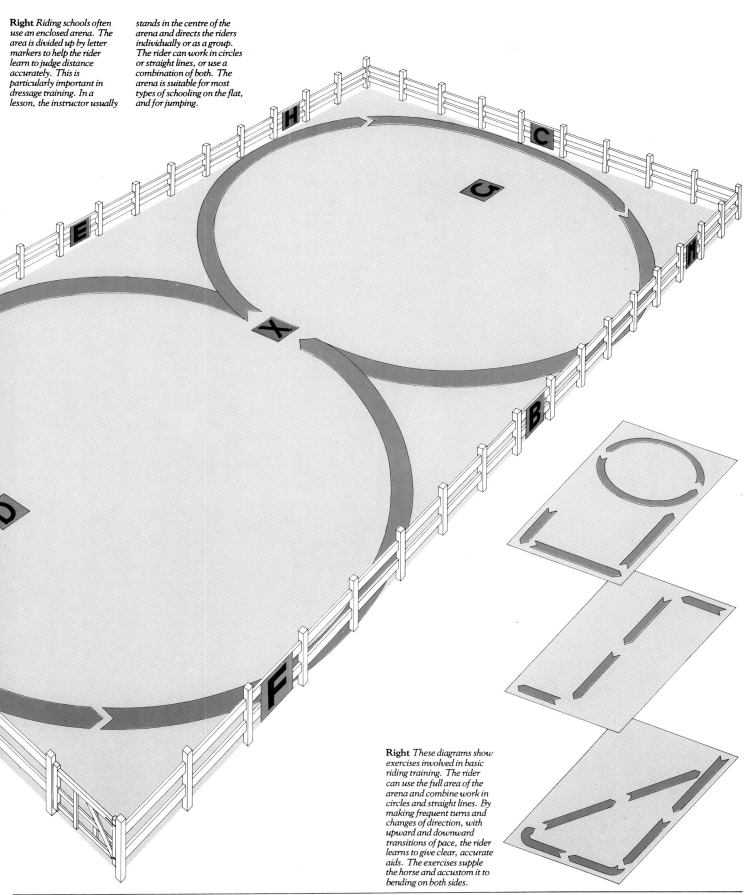

Right *Riding schools often use an enclosed arena. The area is divided up by letter markers to help the rider learn to judge distance accurately. This is particularly important in dressage training. In a lesson, the instructor usually stands in the centre of the arena and directs the riders individually or as a group. The rider can work in circles or straight lines, or use a combination of both. The arena is suitable for most types of schooling on the flat, and for jumping.*

Right *These diagrams show exercises involved in basic riding training. The rider can use the full area of the arena and combine work in circles and straight lines. By making frequent turns and changes of direction, with upward and downward transitions of pace, the rider learns to give clear, accurate aids. The exercises supple the horse and accustom it to bending on both sides.*

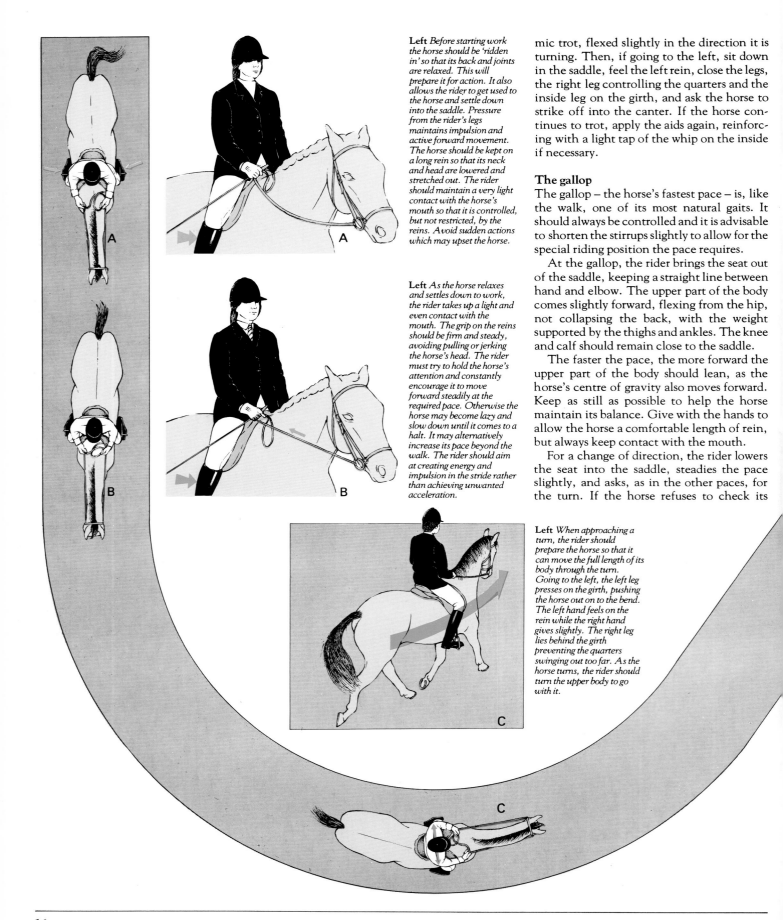

Left *Before starting work the horse should be 'ridden in' so that its back and joints are relaxed. This will prepare it for action. It also allows the rider to get used to the horse and settle down into the saddle. Pressure from the rider's legs maintains impulsion and active forward movement. The horse should be kept on a long rein so that its neck and head are lowered and stretched out. The rider should maintain a very light contact with the horse's mouth so that it is controlled, but not restricted, by the reins. Avoid sudden actions which may upset the horse.*

Left *As the horse relaxes and settles down to work, the rider takes up a light and even contact with the mouth. The grip on the reins should be firm and steady, avoiding pulling or jerking the horse's head. The rider must try to hold the horse's attention and constantly encourage it to move forward steadily at the required pace. Otherwise the horse may become lazy and slow down until it comes to a halt. It may alternatively increase its pace beyond the walk. The rider should aim at creating energy and impulsion in the stride rather than achieving unwanted acceleration.*

Left *When approaching a turn, the rider should prepare the horse so that it can move the full length of its body through the turn. Going to the left, the left leg presses on the girth, pushing the horse out on to the bend. The left hand feels on the rein while the right hand gives slightly. The right leg lies behind the girth preventing the quarters swinging out too far. As the horse turns, the rider should turn the upper body to go with it.*

mic trot, flexed slightly in the direction it is turning. Then, if going to the left, sit down in the saddle, feel the left rein, close the legs, the right leg controlling the quarters and the inside leg on the girth, and ask the horse to strike off into the canter. If the horse continues to trot, apply the aids again, reinforcing with a light tap of the whip on the inside if necessary.

The gallop

The gallop – the horse's fastest pace – is, like the walk, one of its most natural gaits. It should always be controlled and it is advisable to shorten the stirrups slightly to allow for the special riding position the pace requires.

At the gallop, the rider brings the seat out of the saddle, keeping a straight line between hand and elbow. The upper part of the body comes slightly forward, flexing from the hip, not collapsing the back, with the weight supported by the thighs and ankles. The knee and calf should remain close to the saddle.

The faster the pace, the more forward the upper part of the body should lean, as the horse's centre of gravity also moves forward. Keep as still as possible to help the horse maintain its balance. Give with the hands to allow the horse a comfortable length of rein, but always keep contact with the mouth.

For a change of direction, the rider lowers the seat into the saddle, steadies the pace slightly, and asks, as in the other paces, for the turn. If the horse refuses to check its

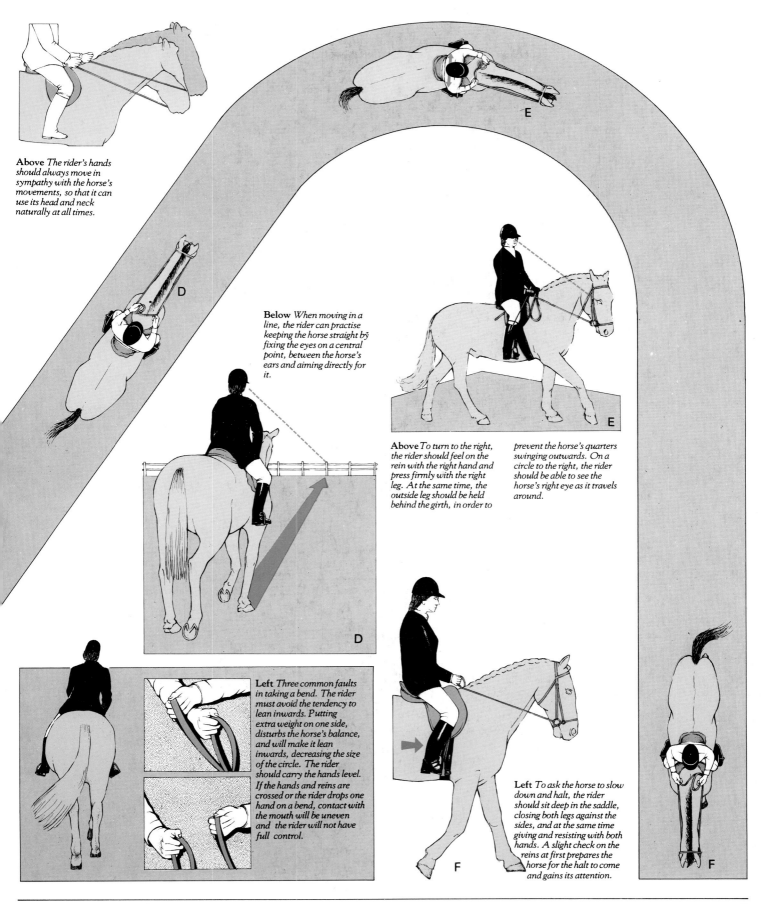

Above *The rider's hands should always move in sympathy with the horse's movements, so that it can use its head and neck naturally at all times.*

Below *When moving in a line, the rider can practise keeping the horse straight by fixing the eyes on a central point, between the horse's ears and aiming directly for it.*

Above *To turn to the right, the rider should feel on the rein with the right hand and press firmly with the right leg. At the same time, the outside leg should be held behind the girth, in order to* *prevent the horse's quarters swinging outwards. On a circle to the right, the rider should be able to see the horse's right eye as it travels around.*

Left *Three common faults in taking a bend. The rider must avoid the tendency to lean inwards. Putting extra weight on one side, disturbs the horse's balance, and will make it lean inwards, decreasing the size of the circle. The rider should carry the hands level. If the hands and reins are crossed or the rider drops one hand on a bend, contact with the mouth will be uneven and the rider will not have full control.*

Left *To ask the horse to slow down and halt, the rider should sit deep in the saddle, closing both legs against the sides, and at the same time giving and resisting with both hands. A slight check on the reins at first prepares the horse for the halt to come and gains its attention.*

pace, the best course of action is to sit upright and turn the horse in a circle. Above all, never pull – the horse will only pull back.

Jumping

Riding over jumps is just as much a matter of confidence as the basic process of learning to ride. All elementary jumping techniques should therefore be learned and practised at the trot, before increasing the pace to a controlled canter. With full confidence and control, jumping comes easily; the basic rule is to aid the horse as much as possible and not to hinder it. When jumping, the stirrups should be slightly shortened.

There are many exercises which can be practised by novice jumpers to help them to learn to jump correctly. For the first lessons, the rider should use a neck strap; this lessens the risk of a nervous pupil pulling on the reins and so jabbing the horse in the mouth with the bit. Jumping without stirrups is also an excellent way of improving balance and developing muscles.

The first step to practise is the approach. Sit well down in the saddle, keeping a very close contact with the horse with thighs, knees and calves, and use the seat and legs to build up impulsion. Support the weight of the body by thighs and ankles - not by the hands - and bring the upper part of the body forward so that it is just off the perpendicular. Never look down, always ahead, and ride for the middle of the obstacle, keeping a light even contact on the reins. The rider must allow the horse freedom of the head and neck.

As the horse starts to leave the ground, bring the hands well down on either side of the neck to allow it to lower and stretch, while bending the body forward from the hip upwards over the centre of gravity. The weight of the body comes slightly out of the saddle. Keep the thighs as close to the horse as possible and the lower leg and feet in the same position as for riding on the flat, making sure that they do not go back in the air.

Once in the air, the rider should give the horse the maximum freedom to complete its jump. Follow the horse's mouth with the hands, but maintain contact. Bring the body well forward from the hip and down close to the horse. As the horse starts to come down to land, begin the return to the normal riding position to balance the animal.

One useful exercise to help achieve a good position is to work with cavalletti in the school. The idea is not to present the rider with real fences, but to simulate them, so that he or she can concentrate on position in the saddle and learn to regulate the horse's stride and direction. The cavalletti can be arranged as a box in the centre of the school, or down one side of it.

Right To rise to the trot the rider leans slightly forward and eases the seat from the saddle to go with the movement of the horse.

Below Three common faults in the trot. In the first diagram, the rider is exaggerating the rise; this stiffens the position and leads to loss of balance. Rising with a hollowed back throws the shoulders forward and the seat back. A slouched back is equally, bad, the spine should be straight.

Below The sitting trot is used particularly during schooling. The rider does not rise to the trot but sits deeply, absorbing the bumps with the small of the back.

Left When making the transition from the trot to a canter, the rider should ensure that the horse leads on the correct leg. This will give a balanced and flowing movement. The rider should sit deeply into the saddle and feel the rein in the direction the horse should lead. The rider squeezes with both legs. The outside leg presses behind the girth – this instructs the horse that its outside hind leg should be first to leave the ground as it changes to the canter. The inside leg is placed on the girth to maintain impulsion. The rider should sit still and follow the natural movement of the canter with the back and hips. The position should be relaxed, but not loose in the saddle. The pace of the canter should always be steady and controlled.

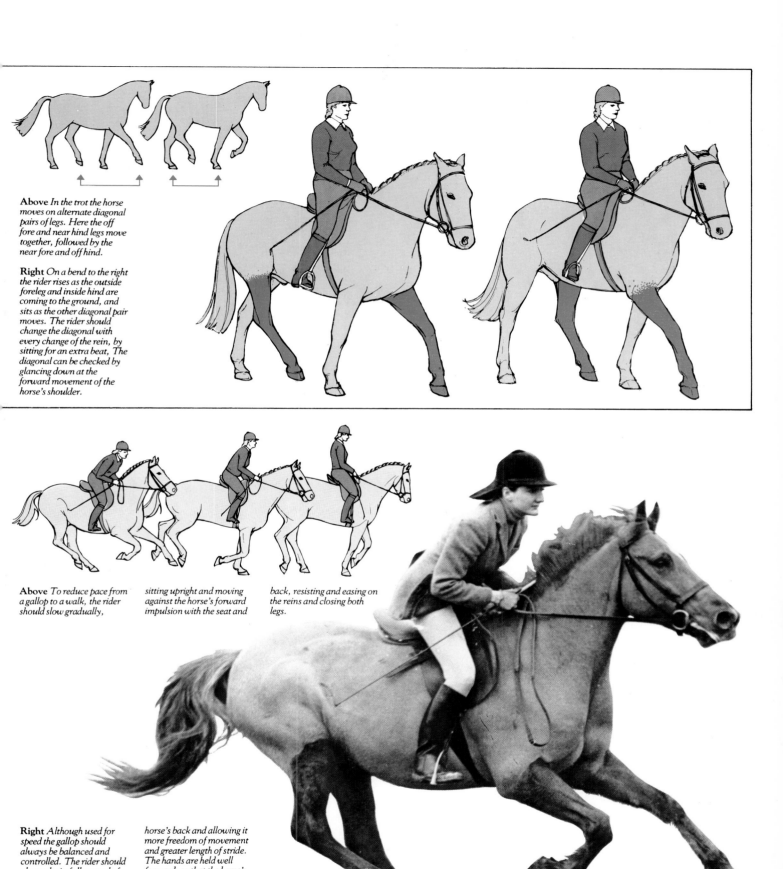

Above *In the trot the horse moves on alternate diagonal pairs of legs. Here the off fore and near hind legs move together, followed by the near fore and off hind.*

Right *On a bend to the right the rider rises as the outside foreleg and inside hind are coming to the ground, and sits as the other diagonal pair moves. The rider should change the diagonal with every change of the rein, by sitting for an extra beat, The diagonal can be checked by glancing down at the forward movement of the horse's shoulder.*

Above *To reduce pace from a gallop to a walk, the rider should slow gradually, sitting upright and moving against the horse's forward impulsion with the seat and back, resisting and easing on the reins and closing both legs.*

Right *Although used for speed the gallop should always be balanced and controlled. The rider should always be in full control of the horse. At the gallop the forward position should be adopted. This means that more weight is taken on the knee and in the heels, relieving the pressure on the horse's back and allowing it more freedom of movement and greater length of stride. The hands are held well forward, so that the horse's neck can stretch out. The gallop is only suited for the open, where there is plenty of space and the ground provides safe going.*

Trot around the school in the sitting-jumping position – this means sitting in the same way as for riding on the flat, but with the upper part of the body bent slightly forward. From any corner of the school, turn to approach the box, coming up into the poised jumping position as you do so. This means that the rider raises the seat out of the saddle, taking the weight on thighs, ankles and heels, without using the reins for support. Then, looking directly ahead, ask the horse to trot through the box. On reaching the other side, return to the original position and trot on around the school on the opposite rein to the one first used.

This exercise enables the rider to practice various angles of approach. It also enables the pupil to control the pace of his or her mount while concentrating on developing the right position in the saddle.

Another, more advanced, exercise with cavalletti helps improve rhythm and timing. Cavalletti are placed at various intervals down one side of the school, one set being combined to create a spread element. The rider soon learns to use the leg and seat aids to lengthen and shorten the horse's stride as necessary.

Through the use of such jumping exercises, a good basic technique can be developed. This is essential before going on to more advanced forms of jumping.

Below *The correct forward jumping position can be practised on a stationary or moving horse. The rider adopts a spring-like position to balance and move with the horse over the jump.*

Body bending forward from hips

Straight back

Head up looking in forward direction

Hands and arms forward and down side of neck

Knees resting on saddle

Shortened stirrups to allow ankles and knees to absorb movement

Weight in heels

Right *Trotting over cavalletti helps the rider develop the forward seat position. This is the correct seat for galloping and jumping.*

Cavalletti are useful for numerous schooling exercises for horse and rider. Schooling over cavalletti is good preparation both for jumping and riding on the flat.

Right *A more advanced exercise is to slightly extend the distance between poles, remove one, or add a small jump. This teaches horse and rider to judge distance and place their strides. The rider should trot over the first poles and then canter in the direction indicated.*

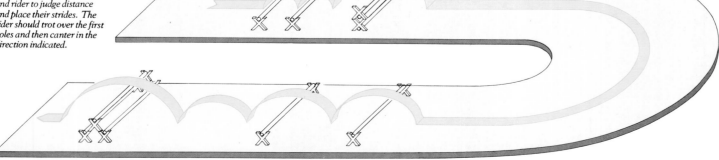

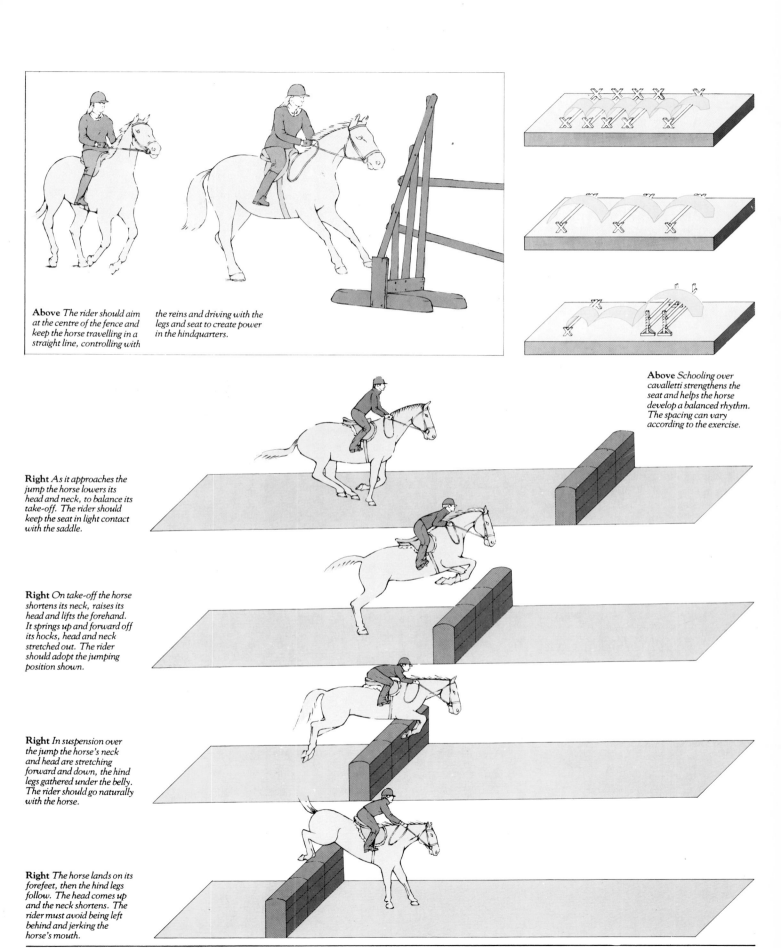

Above *The rider should aim at the centre of the fence and keep the horse travelling in a straight line, controlling with the reins and driving with the legs and seat to create power in the hindquarters.*

Above *Schooling over cavalletti strengthens the seat and helps the horse develop a balanced rhythm. The spacing can vary according to the exercise.*

Right *As it approaches the jump the horse lowers its head and neck, to balance its take-off. The rider should keep the seat in light contact with the saddle.*

Right *On take-off the horse shortens its neck, raises its head and lifts the forehand. It springs up and forward off its hocks, head and neck stretched out. The rider should adopt the jumping position shown.*

Right *In suspension over the jump the horse's neck and head are stretching forward and down, the hind legs gathered under the belly. The rider should go naturally with the horse.*

Right *The horse lands on its forefeet, then the hind legs follow. The head comes up and the neck shortens. The rider must avoid being left behind and jerking the horse's mouth.*

Looking after the horse

Looking after and caring for a horse or pony is perhaps the greatest responsibility any rider faces. Having learned to ride, many riders aim at eventually having a horse of their own. It is worth remembering, though, that looking after a horse unaided – especially if it is stabled – can be a full-time occupation. One answer is to board the horse out at livery, which can be very expensive. Another is to get someone to help out during the day. Most of the other factors involved, such as feeding, watering, exercising and grooming, are mainly matters of common sense, combined with willingness to ask for and take expert advice whenever necessary.

Horses can either be stabled, kept at grass or the two systems can be combined. This means that the horse can run free during the day and have the shelter of a stable by night – except in hot weather, when the procedure should be reversed. Which system is adopted is a matter of choice, practicality, and the type of horse concerned. Ponies, for example, are usually sturdier and more resilient to extremes of climate than horses, particularly thoroughbreds and part-breds. Some thoroughbreds, for instance, should not be left out over the winter. Nor can a horse being worked hard in, say, competitions be really kept fit enough except by being cared for in a stable. At the very least, it must be fed extra food in the field. The amount of extra feeding required should be worked out using the same guidelines as those for a stabled horse. In the case of a field-kept animal, however, the total amount involved should be divided into three, rather than into four.

The combined system can also be adapted to suit the needs of a rider who is using his or her horse frequently, but cannot spare the time to keep it fully stabled. If the horse is

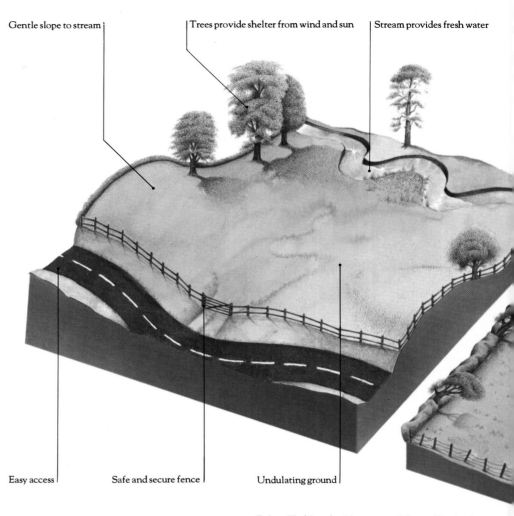

Gentle slope to stream

Trees provide shelter from wind and sun

Stream provides fresh water

Easy access

Safe and secure fence

Undulating ground

Below *Horses may roll to relax after being ridden, or just to deal with an irritating itch. Rolling can also be a symptom of colic, but generally it is simply a sign of pure enjoyment.*

Below *The life cycle of the redworm, or large strongyle. The eggs are dropped in the dung of infected horses. Larvae hatch when conditions are warm and moist to be absorbed during grazing. Inside the horse they* *reach the gut. Piercing the gut wall, they migrate through the internal organs and blood vessels, returning to the gut to mature and lay eggs, which are passed out in the dung to repeat the cycle.*

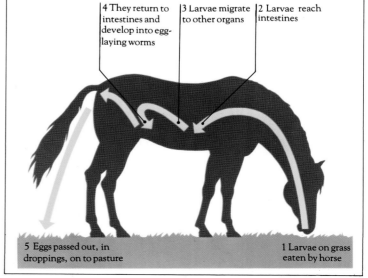

4 They return to intestines and develop into egg-laying worms

3 Larvae migrate to other organs

2 Larvae reach intestines

5 Eggs passed out, in droppings, on to pasture

1 Larvae on grass eaten by horse

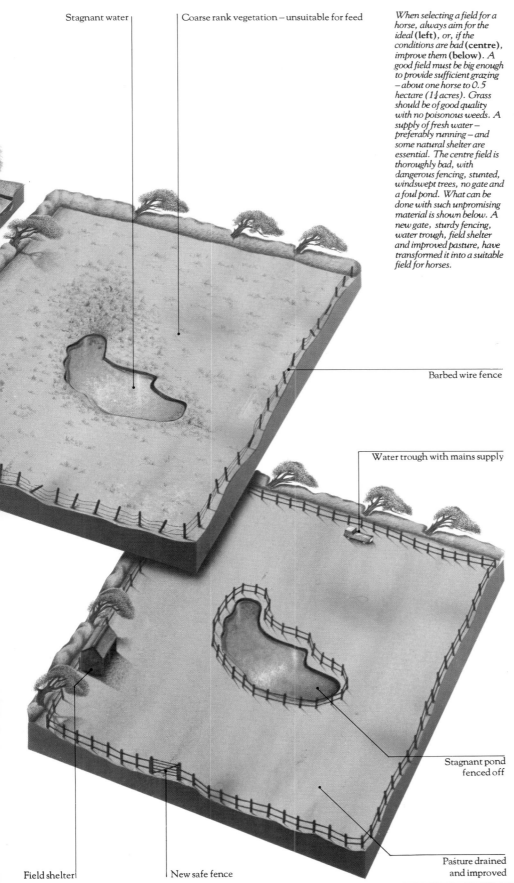

Stagnant water

Coarse rank vegetation – unsuitable for feed

Barbed wire fence

Water trough with mains supply

Stagnant pond fenced off

Pasture drained and improved

Field shelter

New safe fence

When selecting a field for a horse, always aim for the ideal (left), *or, if the conditions are bad* (centre), *improve them* (below). *A good field must be big enough to provide sufficient grazing – about one horse to 0.5 hectare (1¼ acres). Grass should be of good quality with no poisonous weeds. A supply of fresh water – preferably running – and some natural shelter are essential. The centre field is thoroughly bad, with dangerous fencing, stunted, windswept trees, no gate and a foul pond. What can be done with such unpromising material is shown below. A new gate, sturdy fencing, water trough, field shelter and improved pasture, have transformed it into a suitable field for horses.*

being worked regularly in the spring or summer, say, it is a good idea to bring it into the stable first thing in the morning for the first extra feed that will be required. If the horse is to be ridden more than once that day, the same routine is followed as for the stabled horse until the afternoon, when the animal can be turned out for the night. If only one ride is possible, it can be turned out after the second feed, or, if it cannot be exercised at all, it can be turned out after the first.

Keeping a horse at grass

Looking after a horse kept at grass is less time-consuming than looking after one kept in a stable. Among the pluses are the natural vitamins and the exercise the horse gets, but equal responsibility is still demanded from the owner. Statistics show that more accidents happen to horses left unattended in a field than those in a stable. They can kick each other, get tangled up in fences or gates and quickly lose condition either through illness or just plain bad weather. Also, a horse should be visited every day, even if it is not being ridden. Horses are gregarious creatures – ideally, a horse should be kept in company with others – and require affection. Neglect will only make them difficult, if not impossible, to catch.

The ideal field is large – between six and eight acres. It should be undulating, well-drained, securely fenced by a high-grown hedge reinforced by post-and-rail fencing, with a clump of trees at one end and a gravel-bedded stream to provide fresh water. But this situation is often hard to achieve. It is usually considered that about 1 to 1½ acres per pony is adequate, provided that the grass is kept in good condition. Because horses are 'selective grazers' – that is, they pick and choose where and what they eat – a paddock can become 'horse sick'. Some places will be almost bare of grass, while others will be overgrown with the rank, coarse grasses the horses have found unpalatable. In addition, the ground will almost certainly be infested with parasites, the eggs of which horses pass in their dung. If action is not taken, the horses are sure to become infected with worms. These fall into two categories, of which roundworms are by far the most important and potentially destructive. Of these, the most dangerous are red worms *(Strongyles)*, which, untreated, can lead to severe loss of condition. Even though the horse is well-fed, it looks thin and 'poor', with a staring coat; in the worst cases, anaemia may develop or indigestion, colic and enteritis.

As far as an infected horse is concerned, the treatment is regular worming, but it is far better to tackle the problem at source by making sure that the field is maintained properly. A large field should be subdivided so that one area can be rested while another is being grazed. Ideally, sheep or cattle should be introduced on the the resting areas, as they will eat the tall grasses the horses have rejected. They will also help reduce worm infestation, as their digestive juices kill horse worms. Harrowing is also essential as it aerates the soil, encouraging new grass to grow, and also scatters the harmful dung. Failing this, the manure must be collected at least twice a week and transferred to a compost heap.

Mowing after grazing, coupled with the use of a balanced fertilizer, also helps keep a field in good condition, but horses should not be returned to their grazing too soon after it has been so treated. If in doubt, allow three weeks.

Bots are another problem for field-kept horses, for which veterinary treatment is necessary.

Food, water and shelter
All grassland is composed of a mixture of grasses and other plants. Some have little nutritional value, though the horse may well like them, but the three most important are Perennial Rye Grass *(Lolium perennae)*, Cocksfoot *(Dactylis glomerata)* and Timothy *(Phleum pratense)*. Some White Clover *(Trifolium repens)* is useful, but beware of a heavily-clovered pasture. This may prove too rich and lead to digestive problems.

Even if clover is not present, grass itself can cause problems. This is especially the case in the spring when excessive greed can lead a horse to put on too much weight, and sometimes to the painful disease called laminitis, or founder. Also, a horse or pony can only exist on grass alone for the summer months – from about the end of April to the beginning of September. By October, supplementary feeding becomes essential. Start off with hay and then provide oats or beans, if required. The more refined the breed, the more extra feeding that will be necessary.

Water is another essential; field-kept horses must have easy access to a plentiful supply of fresh water. Remember that a horse drinks about 35 litres (8 gal) a day. If the water supply is in the form of a stream, check that it can be reached by means of a gentle slope; if the banks are steep or muddy, it is safer to fence the stream off and provide a water trough instead. Similarly, always fence off stagnant pools and ponds.

The most convenient form of trough is one connected to a mains water supply, controlled either by a tap or automatic valve. Custom-made troughs are on the market, but cheaper alternatives are an old domestic cistern or bath. Remember to remove all sharp

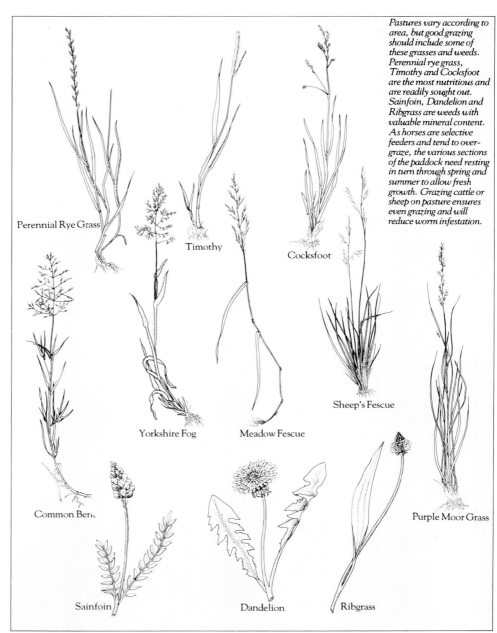

Pastures vary according to area, but good grazing should include some of these grasses and weeds. Perennial rye grass, Timothy and Cocksfoot are the most nutritious and are readily sought out. Sainfoin, Dandelion and Ribgrass are weeds with valuable mineral content. As horses are selective feeders and tend to overgraze, the various sections of the paddock need resting in turn through spring and summer to allow fresh growth. Grazing cattle or sheep on pasture ensures even grazing and will reduce worm infestation.

Perennial Rye Grass

Timothy

Cocksfoot

Yorkshire Fog

Meadow Fescue

Sheep's Fescue

Common Bent

Purple Moor Grass

Sainfoin

Dandelion

Ribgrass

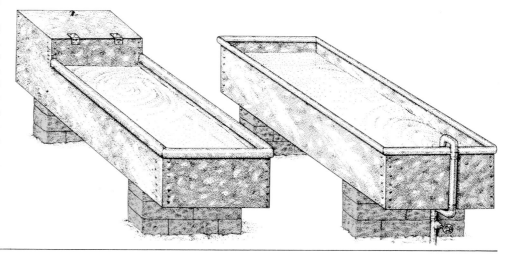

Left *A shelter is an essential addition to any field – even one with trees and hedges – as horses need one to escape from wind and cold in winter. In summer it provides shade, coolness and protection from insects. In cold or wet weather, hay can be conveniently fed in a rack or hay-net within the shelter.*

Below *Post-and-rail fencing made of good timber is the safest kind. It must be firm and strongly built. Trees and hedges provide a natural wind-break and shelter from the rain. They also shade the horse from the sun.*

Fencing and gates

Sound and strong fencing is essential for safety. A fence must be high enough to prevent horses from jumping over it – 1.3m (3ft 9in) is the absolute minimum. Bars must also be fitted; two rails are usually adequate for containing horses, with the bottom one about 4.5cm (18in) from the ground. Small ponies, however, can wriggle through incredibly small gaps, so a third or even a fourth rail should be added for them. This type of fencing is known as post-and-rail, or 'Man O' War'.

Of all the types of fencing available, timber is the safest but most expensive. Hedges run a close second, but should be regularly checked, as otherwise a determined pony might well push his way through. Gaps can be reinforced with timber, but avoid filling a gap with wire. Concealed by a hedge in summer, it could be hard for a horse to see and so could lead to accidental injury. Stone walls are also attractive, but, they, too, will need regular checking, especially after a hard winter when frost may have loosened the mortar.

However, wire is perfectly adequate as fencing on its own, as long as the correct type of wire is used. Avoid barbed wire, chicken mesh or sheep wire and use a plain heavy gauge galvinized wire instead. For safety and effectiveness, the strands must be stretched so that they are evenly taut and then stapled to the inside of the posts. Strong stretcher posts, should be positioned at regular intervals. Check regularly for signs of weakness, such as loose posts, broken wires or sprung staples. If each strand of wire ends in an eye bolt attached to the end posts, the wire can be tightened from time to time.

Gates are another safety factor. The only criterion is that they should be easy for people to open and close, but that it should be impossible for the horse to do so. A five-

projections, such as taps, and to give the inside a thorough cleaning before putting into use. If there is no piped water supply, use a hose or fill the trough with buckets.

Buckets alone are totally insufficient. A horse can easily drink a whole bucket of water at one go, and, in any case, a bucket can all too easily be kicked over. Daily checks of the water supply are vital, especially in winter, when ice may form and must be broken. A child's rubber ball left floating on the surface of a trough will help to keep the water ice-free, except when frosts are severe, when the ice must be broken daily.

Winter and summer also bring the problem of shelter. From a horse's point of view, the worst elements are wind, rain and sun. Even if the field possesses a natural windbreak, an artificial shelter is a good addition. It need not be complicated – a three-sided shed the size of a large loose box is usually adequate. Make sure that the open side does not face the sun.

Far left *Self-filling trough with automatic valve in enclosed section and* **left** *trough with inlet pipe close-fitted and tap recessed beneath. Both are of safe design with no sharp edges or projections. Site a trough on well-drained ground to avoid churned mud and away from the falling leaves of trees. Troughs should be emptied and cleaned regularly. If ice forms in the winter it should be broken daily.*

Right *Suitable types of fencing. From the left: post and rail, post and wire, rail and wire combined and dry stone wall. Check the tautness of wire fences regularly and inspect walls for damage after frosts.*

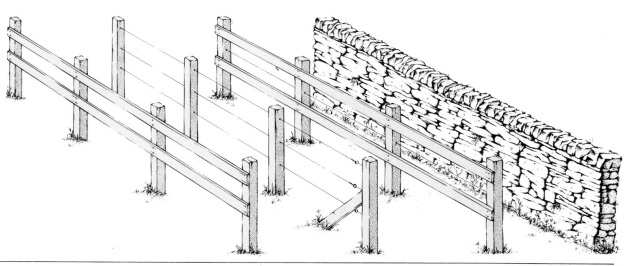

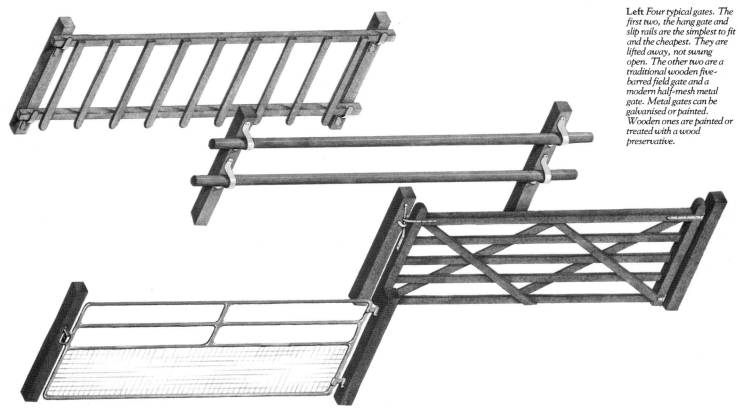

Left *Four typical gates. The first two, the hang gate and slip rails are the simplest to fit and the cheapest. They are lifted away, not swung open. The other two are a traditional wooden five-barred field gate and a modern half-mesh metal gate. Metal gates can be galvanised or painted. Wooden ones are painted or treated with a wood preservative.*

barred farm gate, hung just clear of the ground so that it swings freely when un-latched, is ideal. It should be fitted with either a self-closing latch, or with a simple chain fitted with a snap lock and fastened to the latching post. Slip rails and hang-gates are cheaper alternatives.

'Turning out', exercise and grooming

Before a pony or horse is turned out into a field, always check it carefully. Inspect the gate and fencing, strengthening any weak points. Make certain that there are no poisonous plants either in the field or within reach of the fence. See that there is an adequate supply of water, and check that there are no man-made hazards, such as broken bottles, tin cans and plastic bags lying about, which could injure the horse; a pony can die if it swallows a plastic bag, for exam-ple. Have any rabbit holes filled in to avoid the risk of a cantering horse catching its feet in one, falling, and perhaps breaking a leg.

When you are satisfied with the state of the field, turn the horse out. If it is not to be ridden for some time, say over the winter, have the shoes removed. This will lessen the danger of injury in the event of any kicking contest with other horses kept in the field.

Before exercising, always check the horse for cuts, bruises and other injuries. This pro-cedure should also be carried out during the daily visits. Pick out the feet, noting the condition of the shoes. Also check the teeth

regularly. Left unattended, they can develop rough edges, which make eating difficult. If this happens, they will need to be filed.

Remember, too, that the horse will be in what is known as 'grass condition'. Its soft muscles and its extra layers of fat will make it incapable of any prolonged period of hard work, without sweating heavily and exhibit-ing other signs of distress. Forcing a horse to do so will only damage wind and limbs. If, as at the start of the school holidays, say, the horse is being ridden frequently for the first time in some months, it is a good idea to start a supplementary feeding programme a few weeks before, as grass is not a high-energy food. In any case, exercise should always be gradual, slowly building up from walking to a full exercise programme.

After exercise, the horse may well be swea-ty, particularly if the animal has a long, shaggy coat. It is best to turn it out im-mediately and not to wait until the sweat has completely dried, or there is the danger of colds or, in extreme cases, colic. Conversely, in winter remember that the grease in a horse's coat helps to keep it warm, so restrict after-exercise grooming to remove any mud. A clipped horse should always wear a New Zealand rug in the field in the winter.

Groom with a dandy brush, taking care to get rid of all dried and caked mud and any sweat marks. Groom the mane and tail with a body brush and, finally, sponge out eyes, nostrils and dock.

Gate fastenings must be impossible for horses to open, but simple for human beings. Here are three secure kinds. **Top** *A simple catch with a lug* *held in a notch.* **Centre** *A catch with a release mechanism.* **Below** *A spring catch with a bar held forward against a retaining hook.*

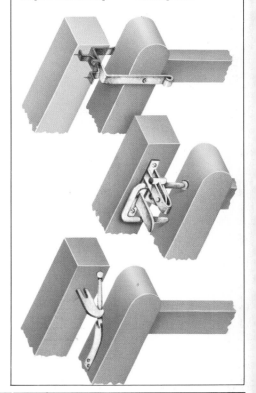

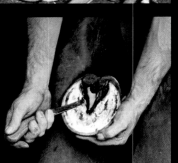

A farrier displays his skill in hot shoeing. After cutting clenches he removes the old shoe with pincers (above) and trims away overgrown horn with a drawing knife (right). The farrier's forge and tools are seen (below left). The new shoe is forged (top right) and fitted hot to reveal unevenness (below right). The new clenches are smoothed off with a rasp after fitting (extreme right).

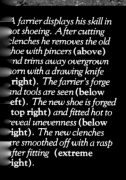

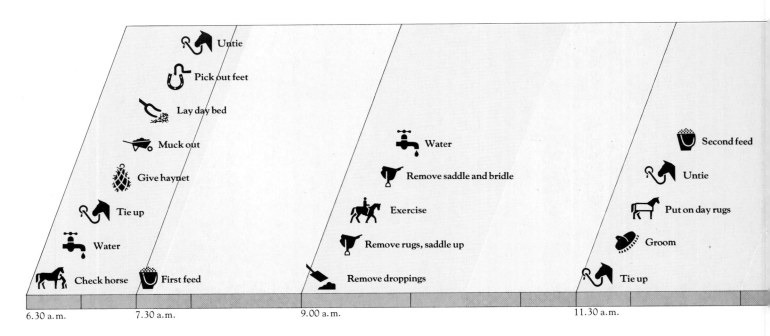

Untie
Pick out feet
Lay day bed
Muck out
Give haynet
Tie up
Water
Check horse   First feed

Water
Remove saddle and bridle
Exercise
Remove rugs, saddle up
Remove droppings

Second feed
Untie
Put on day rugs
Groom
Tie up

6.30 a.m.   7.30 a.m.   9.00 a.m.   11.30 a.m.

Shoeing the horse

Any horse being ridden regularly on a hard surface, such as a road, must be shod, or the wall of the hoof will be worn down quicker than it can grow. This will cause friction, soreness and lameness. Hardy ponies, working lightly and solely on grass, can do without shoes, but their hooves should still be looked at regularly by a blacksmith.

Inspections should take place at regular four to six week intervals. The signs that a horse needs to be reshod are a loose shoe; one that has been 'cast' (lost); a shoe wearing thin; one in which the clenches (securing nails) have risen and stand out from the wall; and if the foot is overlong and out of shape.

Horses can be either hot-shod or cold-shod. In hot-shoeing, the red hot shoe is shaped to the exact size of the hoof. In the latter, the shoes are pre–cast and fitted cold. Whichever method is used by the blacksmith, always check the following points after shoeing has been completed.

Make sure that the shoe has been made to fit the foot – not vice versa. Check that the shoe is suitable for the work you want the horse to do, and that the weight of the shoes is in the right proportion to the horse's size.

As a rough guide, a set of shoes for a horse should usually weigh around 2kg (4½lb). Look at the heel and toe of the foot to make sure that its length has been reduced evenly. See that the foot is in contact with the ground. Check that the right size and number of nails have been used and the clenches are correctly formed, in line and the right distance up the wall. Finally, make sure the clip fits securely and that there is no gap showing between the newly-fitted shoe and the hoof.

Fixtures and fittings

The basic rule to follow is the fewer fittings the better, to minimize the risk of possible injury. The only essential is a means of tying the horse up. Normally, this consists of two rings, fixed to bolts which pass right through the stable wall. One ring should be at waist

Mucking out is the first job done each morning in the stable. Soiled straw and dung are separated from the cleaner portions of the night bedding by tossing with a fork. The cleaner straw is then heaped at the back of the stall to be used again.

The soiled straw and droppings are put into a barrow for removal to the manure heap. In fine weather much of the night bedding can be carried outside to air in the sun. This will freshen it up, restore its springiness and make it last longer.

When the bulk of soiled straw has been removed and the cleaner straw reserved, the floor should be swept clean of remaining dirt. It should be left bare to dry off and air for a while. The clean straw is then spread as a soft floor-covering for the day.

The soiled straw and dung are tossed on the manure heap. Take care to throw the muck right on to the top of the heap, as a neatly built heap decomposes more efficiently. Beat the heap down with a shovel after each load to keep it firm and dense.

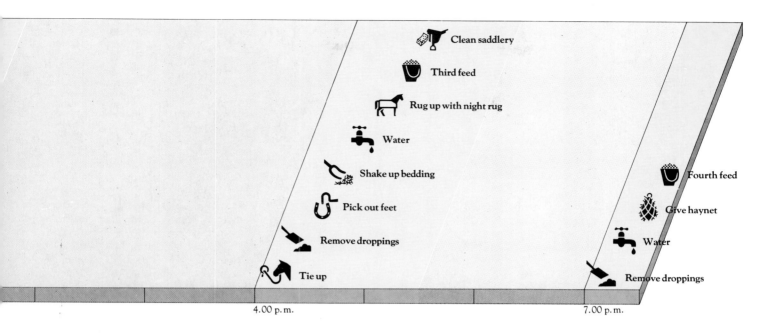

Clean saddlery

Third feed

Rug up with night rug

Water

Shake up bedding

Pick out feet

Remove droppings

Tie up

Fourth feed

Give haynet

Water

Remove droppings

4.00 p.m.   7.00 p.m.

Above *The daily routine for a fully-stabled horse, showing the order of work and the times at which different tasks are carried out. The feeding schedule will vary according to the size and work-load of individual horses. Many owners prefer the less time-consuming combined system, in which horses spend part of the day out in the field.*

height and the other at head height. All other fittings and fixtures are a matter of individual preference.

Fixed mangers positioned at breast level and secured either along a wall or in a corner of the loose box are found in many stables. They should be fitted with lift-out bowls to facilitate cleaning and have well-rounded corners. The space beneath should be boxed in to prevent the horse from injuring itself on the manger's rim – this space makes a good storage place for a grooming kit. However, a container on the floor, which is heavy enough not to be knocked over and which can be removed as soon as the horse has finished its feed is adequate.

Fitted hay racks are found in some stables, but they are not really advisable. They force the horse to eat with its head held unnaturally high and hayseeds may fall into its eyes. The best way of feeding hay is to use a haynet. It is also the least wasteful, as haynets permit accurate weighing. The net should always be hung well clear of the ground and be fastened with a quick-release knot to one of the tying-up rings.

Water is as essential to the horse in the stable as for a horse in the field. Automatic watering bowls are one way of providing a constant supply – but never position them too close to the haynet and manger, or they may get blocked by surplus food. Buckets are satisfactory, provided, again, that the bucket

is heavy enough not to be accidentally upset. Use of a bucket means that it is possible to control the amount of water the horse drinks – important after exercise, for instance, when a 'heated' horse must not drink too much – and also to check how much it is drinking more easily. This is especially useful in cases of suspected illness.

Stable routine

The daily programme for looking after a stabled horse takes up a great deal of time. All the stages have to be carried out, though some, such as the number of feeds, will vary from case to case. Skimping will only lead to problems later.

1. Tie up the horse and check over for injuries which may have occurred during the night. Replenish its water, if necessary, and fill the haynet. Muck out the stable. Quarter the horse thoroughly. Pick out feet with a hoof pick. Lay the day bed.
2. First feed.
3. Allow the horse time to digest – at least 1¼ hours – and then saddle up and exercise. On returning to the stable, refill water bucket and remove droppings.
4. Tie up and groom thoroughly. Put on day rug (blanket) if used. Check water again and refill the haynet. Give the second feed.
5. Pick out feet again and remove droppings. Shake up bedding, replace the day rug (blanket) with a night rug, and replenish water.
6. Third feed. Clean tack.
7. Remove droppings, and lay the night-bed. Replenish the water and re-fill the haynet. Final feed. Put on a night rug (blanket), if worn.

The only way of short-circuiting this

routine is to adopt the combined system of care. This has considerable advantages in time and labour, but is not suited to all horses, especially those being worked hard. Otherwise, board or livery is the only alternative. Some riding schools offer what is termed half-livery; this means that the horse gets free board in exchange for use as a hack. The risk is that the horse may be roughly treated by inexperienced riders even in a supervised lesson. Full livery is extremely expensive; in the UK it can cost as much as £30 a week. In either case, always check that the stable you choose is officially approved by a recognized riding authority.

The principal areas of a horse-owner's day, however, are not as complex as they seem. They can be broken down into various tasks, all of which are relatively simple to carry out.

Bedding down and mucking out

The purpose of bedding is to give the horse something comfortable to lie on, insulate the box, absorb moisture and prevent the horse's legs jarring on the hard stable floor. It must be kept clean – hence the daily task of mucking out. This is usually done first thing in the morning, and, with practice, can be carried out quite quickly.

Straw is the best possible bedding material, though other kinds can be substituted. Wheat straw is excellent, because it is absorbent and lasts well. Barley straw may contain awns, which can irritate the horse's skin. Oat straw should be avoided, because horses tend to eat it and it tends to become saturated.

Of the substitutes, peat makes a soft, well-insulated bed; it is also the least inflammable of all bedding materials. However, it is heavy to work. Damp patches and droppings must

Wheat straw (left) makes ideal bedding. It is warm, comfortable, easy to handle and absorbent. Wood shavings (centre) make cheaper bedding and are often laid on a base of sawdust to reduce dampness. Droppings have to be removed frequently. Peat moss (right) makes a soft bed, but tends to be dusty when first laid down and needs frequent raking.

be removed at once, replacing with fresh peat when necessary. The whole bed requires forking over and raking every day, as the material can cause foot problems if it becomes damp and compacted.

Wood shavings and sawdust are usually cheap but can be difficult to get rid of. Both need to be checked carefully to see that they do not contain nails, screws, paint, oil or other foreign matter. Wood shavings can be used alone, but note that they can cause foot problems if they become damp and compacted. Sawdust is best used in combination with other materials.

There are two types of bed – the day bed and the night bed. The first is a thin layer of bedding laid on the floor for use during the day; the second is thicker and more comfortable for use at night. With materials such as peat or wood shavings, laying the bed is very simple. Just empty the contents of the sack on the floor and rake them level, building up the material slightly higher around the walls to minimize draughts.

Laying a straw bed requires slightly more skill. As the straw will be compacted in the bale, it has to be shaken up so that the stalks separate, and laid so that the finished bed is aerated, springy and free from lumps. A pitchfork is best for the purpose.

Some owners prefer the deep litter method of bedding, where fresh straw is added to the existing bed every day, removing only droppings and sodden straw beforehand. After a time, the bed becomes as much as two feet deep, well-compacted below and soft and resilient on the surface. At the end of a month, the whole bed is removed and restarted. This method should be used only in loose boxes with first-rate drainage. In addition, the feet must be picked out regularly, as otherwise there is a major risk of disease.

Feeding and fodder

Heredity has given the horse a very small stomach for its size and the food it eats takes up to 48 hours to pass through the digestive system. This system is in itself complex. It depends not only on the right amounts of food at the correct time for smoothness of

Laying a night bed of straw requires some skill. First (above) clean straw saved from the day bed is tossed and shaken well with a pitchfork before being spread evenly over the floor as a foundation.

Next new straw is taken from the compressed bale and shaken well to free the stalks and make the bed springy. The floor must be thickly and evenly covered to encourage the horse to lie down.

Last the straw is banked up higher and more thickly around the sides of the box. This cuts down draughts, keeps the horse warmer and gives the animal extra protection from injury during the night.

operation, but also on an adequate supply of water and plenty of exercise. In the wild, horses drink twice a day, usually at dawn and dusk. In between, their day is divided into periods of grazing, rest and exercise. Field-kept horses can duplicate this pattern to some extent, but stabled horses cannot do so.

It is essential to follow a basic set of feeding rules. Otherwise the horse's sensitive digestion may well be upset, encouraging the risks of indigestion, impaction, formation of gas in the stomach or sudden colic attacks.

The basic rules are to feed little and often, with plenty of bulk food – grass or hay – and according to the work you expect the horse to do. Make no sudden change in the type of food, or in the routine of feeding, once the diet and time has been established. Always water the horse before feeding, so that undigested food is not washed out of the stomach. Never work a horse hard straight after feeding or if its stomach is full of grass. Let it digest for $1\frac{1}{4}$ hours or so, otherwise the full stomach will impair breathing. Similarly, never feed a horse immediately after hard work, when it will be 'heated'.

The staple diet of the horse is grass, or, in the case of a stabled horse, hay. The best type is seed hay, usually a mixture of rye grass and clover, which is specially grown as part of a crop-rotation programme. Meadow grass, also commonly used, comes from permanent pasture and so can vary in quality. The best way of judging this is by appearance, smell and age. Hay should smell sweet, be slightly greenish in colour and at least six months old. Blackened, mouldy or wet hay should never be used as fodder.

Of the other types of hay, clover is too rich to be fed to a horse on its own, and the same rule applies to alfalfa, or lucerne, common in the USA and Canada. Alfalfa is extremely rich in protein, so feed small quantities until you can judge how much is needed.

Concentrates for work

Ponies and horses in regular, hard work need additional food to keep them in a fit, hard-muscled condition. In other words, they need energy rather than fatness. This is provided by the feeding of concentrated foodstuffs, usually known as 'short' or 'hard' feeds. Of these, the best is oats, which can be bruised, crushed or rolled to aid digestion. Manufactured horse cubes or pellets are a useful alternative.

Oats have no equal as a natural high protein, energy-giving food and are an essential part of the diet for all horses in work. Good quality oats are plump and short, and pale gold, silver grey or dark chocolate in colour. They should have a hard, dry feel and no sour smell. Take care, however, not to feed to much, or a horse may speedily become unmanageable. This caution applies particularly to children's ponies, which are often better off without oats at all.

Cubes and pellets are manufactured from various grains and also usually contain some grass meal, sweetners such as molasses or treacle, extra vitamins and minerals. Their nutritional value is about two-thirds that of oats, but they are less heating and so ideal for ponies. Their chief advantage is that they provide a balanced diet on their own, as they do not have to be mixed with other foodstuffs. However, they are expensive.

Other grains can be used in addition or as alternatives to oats, but they are all of lesser quality. Flaked maize (corn) is used in many parts of the world as a staple feed. It is high in energy value, but low in protein and mineral content. Like oats, it can be heating for ponies and is usually fed to animals in slow, regular work, such as riding school hacks. Boiled barley helps to fatten up a horse or pony in poor condition and is a useful addition to the diet of a stale, or overworked horse. Beans, too, are nutritious but, again, because of their heating effect, they should be fed sparingly, either whole, split or boiled.

Other useful foods

Bran makes a useful addition to a horse's diet, as it helps provide roughage. It is either fed dry mixed up with oats – the combined mixture should be slightly dampened – or in the form of a mash. This is a good 'pick me up' for a tired or sick horse. The mash is made by mixing $\frac{2}{3}$ of a bucket of bran with $\frac{1}{3}$ of boiling water and is fed to the horse as soon as it is cool enough to eat. Always remove any remains, as the mash can quickly go rancid. Oatmeal gruel is an alternative. This is made by pouring boiling water on to porridge oats and leaving to cool. Use enough water to make the gruel thin enough in consistency for the horse to drink.

Linseed, prepared as a jelly, mash or tea, is fed to horses in winter to improve condition

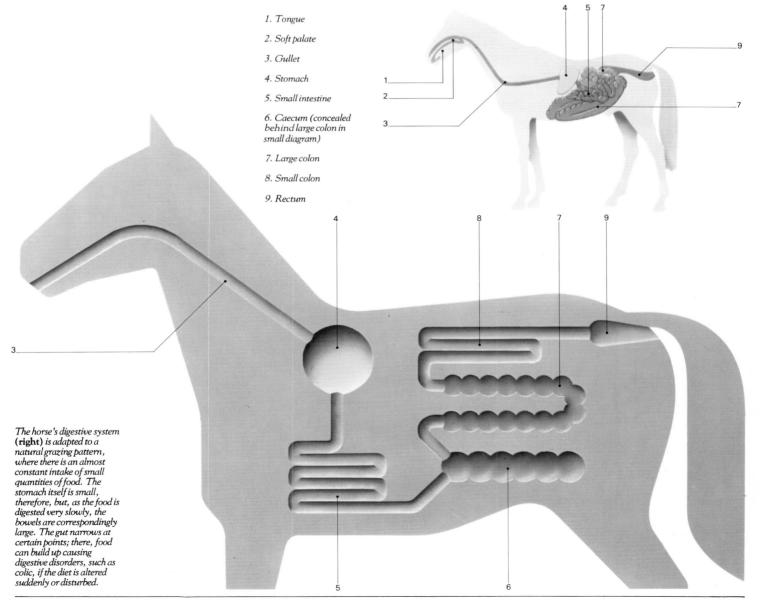

1. Tongue

2. Soft palate

3. Gullet

4. Stomach

5. Small intestine

6. Caecum (concealed behind large colon in small diagram)

7. Large colon

8. Small colon

9. Rectum

The horse's digestive system (**right**) is adapted to a natural grazing pattern, where there is an almost constant intake of small quantities of food. The stomach itself is small, therefore, but, as the food is digested very slowly, the bowels are correspondingly large. The gut narrows at certain points; there, food can build up causing digestive disorders, such as colic, if the diet is altered suddenly or disturbed.

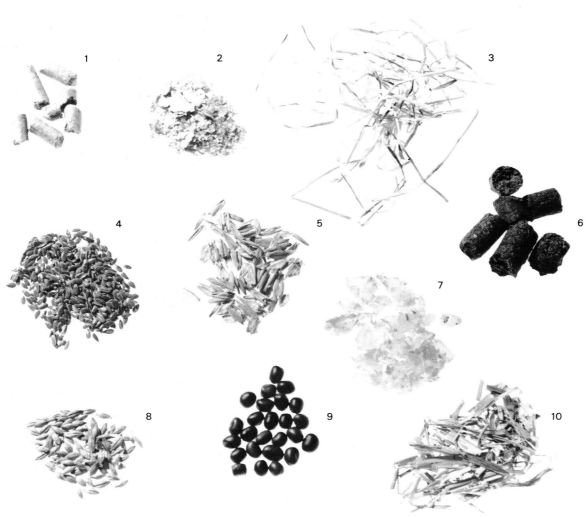

Left *Basic concentrated foods are an essential part of the diet for horses in hard, regular work. 1 Pony nuts are a compound food which contain all essential nutrients and can be fed, dry, instead of oats. Add chaff or bran to aid digestion. 2 Bran is rich in protein, vitamin B and salt. Fed as a mash, or slightly damp, with oats, it has a laxative effect. 3 Hay contains all nutrients needed to keep horses fit, if at grass, or only lightly worked. 4 Linseed fed as jelly, tea or cake has a high oil content and laxative properties. It is good for conditioning as it makes the coat glossy. 5 Oats are a balanced, nutritious and easily digested food, high in energy-giving carbohydrate, Vitamin B and muscle-building protein. They are fed whole, bruised or crushed. 6 Sugar beet cubes provide bulk for horses in slow work. They must be soaked before use, or will swell in stomach and cause colic. There is also a great danger of the horse choking. 7 Maize, fed flaked for digestibility, is energising, but low in protein and minerals. It contains vitamin A. 8 Barley, unsuitable for horses in long, fast work, is fed, boiled, as a general conditioner; it should be crushed if fed raw. It contains vitamin B. 9 Peas are protein-rich; feed them sparingly for energy or conditioning. 10 Chaff has little food value but gives bulk and helps mastication. Add 450g (1lb) to every feed ration.*

and to give gloss to the coat. It must be soaked then well cooked to kill the poisonous enzyme present in the raw plant. Let the mix cool before giving it to the horse. Dried sugar beet is another good conditioner, because of its high energy content. Most horses like it because of its sweetness. It must be always soaked in water overnight before it is added to a feed. If fed dry, the beet is likely to cause severe colic, as it swells dramatically when wet.

Roots, such as carrots, turnips and swedes, again help condition and are also of particular value to delicate or fussy feeders. Always wash the roots first and then slice them into finger-shaped pieces. Small round slices may cause a pony to choke.

Molasses or black treacle can be mixed with food to encourage a finicky feeder. In any case, all feeds ideally should contain about ·45kg (1lb) of chaff – chopped hay. Chaff has practically no nutritional content, but it does ensure that the horse chews its food properly, so helping to minimize the risk

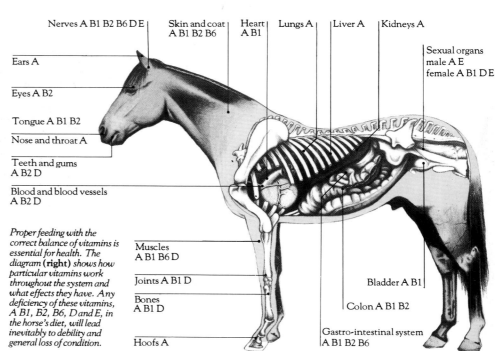

Proper feeding with the correct balance of vitamins is essential for health. The diagram (right) shows how particular vitamins work throughout the system and what effects they have. Any deficiency of these vitamins, A B1, B2, B6, D and E, in the horse's diet, will lead inevitably to debility and general loss of condition.

Nerves A B1 B2 B6 D E

Skin and coat A B1 B2 B6

Heart A B1

Lungs A

Liver A

Kidneys A

Sexual organs male A E female A B1 D E

Ears A

Eyes A B2

Tongue A B1 B2

Nose and throat A

Teeth and gums A B2 D

Blood and blood vessels A B2 D

Muscles A B1 B6 D

Joints A B1 D

Bones A B1 D

Bladder A B1

Colon A B1 B2

Gastro-intestinal system A B1 B2 B6

Hoofs A

of indigestion. It also acts as an abrasive on teeth. Finally, a salt or mineral lick – left in the manger – is essential for all stabled horses. Field-kept animals usually take in an adequate amount of salt during grazing, but a lick is also a good safeguard.

Vitamins and minerals

An adequate supply of vitamins and minerals is vital in addition to the required amounts of carbohydrates, proteins and fat. Vitamins A, B1, B2, B6, D and E are all essential; otherwise the horse's resistance to disease will certainly be lessened, and actual disease may well result. Normally, good-class hay and grass, bran and carrots will contain most of the vitamins a horse needs; oats, barley, flaked maize and sugar beet pulp are also all useful. Vitamin D, however, can only be artificially administered through cod liver oil, or left to the action of sunlight on the natural oil in the coat.

The absence of a sufficient supply of minerals can be even more serious than a lack of vitamins, especially in the case of a young horse. The essential minerals required are: calcium and phosphorus, for the formation of healthy teeth and bones; sodium, sodium chloride (salt) and potassium, for regulation of the amount of body fluids; iron and copper, vital for the formation of haemoglobin in the blood to prevent anaemia; while magnesium, manganese, cobalt, zinc and iodine are all necessary. Magnesium aids skeletal and muscular development; manganese is needed for both the bone structure and for reproduction; zinc and cobalt stimulate growth; while iodine is particularly important in control of the thyroid gland.

However, of all these minerals, the most important is salt. This is why it is vital to provide a horse with a salt lick in either stable of field.

As with vitamins, the chief source of these minerals is grass or hay, together with the other foods mentioned above. However, if the horse needs extra vitamins and minerals, always take the advice of a vet first – an excess of vitamins or minerals can be as dangerous as an underdose. These are many suitable proprietary products on the market. These usually come in the form of liquid, powders and pellets, designed to be mixed in with other food for ease of feeding.

Signs of lack of vitamins are usually seen on the skin and coat; examination of the teeth, gums and eyes can also give warning of possible deficiency. But, with sensible and controlled feeding, the problem should not arise.

Quantities to feed

There is no hard and fast guide to the exact

A separate food store is essential. It should be clean, dry and near to the water supply. Foodstuffs kept in the stable can easily become spoiled or contaminated. The horse is a fastidious feeder, and musty or dusty food, as well as being un-appetizing, may be harmful. The simple food store (below) provides a clean, secure and compact area where foodstuffs can be measured out and mixed. Large establishments often keep a chaff cutter and an oat crusher. Scales are also useful to check the weight of filled haynets periodically.

Foodstuffs should be kept in separate bins, or sections of one large bin, and only mixed at feedtime. A scoop is used to measure out each ration. Where several horses are kept a check list for feeding should be pinned up near the bins so that each receives its appropriate diet.

The feed can be dampened slightly with water before being mixed by hand in a bucket and then fed to horse. Grain keeps fresh and dry in galvanised bins. These should have close-fitting lids to keep out vermin and heavy enough to prevent a horse from raising them.

amounts of food a horse should be fed, as much depends on the type and size of horse and the work it is expected to do. However, as far as a stabled horse is concerned, the amount should certainly not be less than the horse would eat if it was grazing freely.

If the horse concerned was 15·2 hands, say, it would eat approximately 26½lbs of grass a day. Bigger horses require an extra 2lbs for every extra 2ins of height; smaller ones need 2lbs less.

With this basic total established, it is possible to plan a feeding programme, varying the amounts of bulk and concentrated food according to the demands being made upon the horse. Taking as an example a lightweight 15·2 hand horse that is being hunted, say, three days a fortnight in addition to other regular work, the emphasis will be on an almost equal balance between concentrates and hay or grass. The horse should be getting some 14lbs of concentrates a day to some 15lbs of hay. If, however, the horse is being lightly worked – or not worked at all – the

amount of hay will rise and the quantities of concentrates diminish.

Remember, too, that most horses feed much better at night, so it is important that the highest proportion of food be given in the final feed of the day. If the horse is being given three feeds a day, for example, the proportions are ten per cent in the morning, thirty per cent at midday and sixty per cent at night.

The best guide of all is simple observation. If a horse is too fat, it will need its rations reduced; if too thin, it will need building up. Always reduce the amount if food is left uneaten.

Exercising the horse

All stabled horses must have regular and adequate exercise. Otherwise they can develop swollen legs, azoturia and colic – and will, in any case be spirited and difficult to manage when ridden. They can also become bored and develop bad habits. The amounts needed vary with the type and

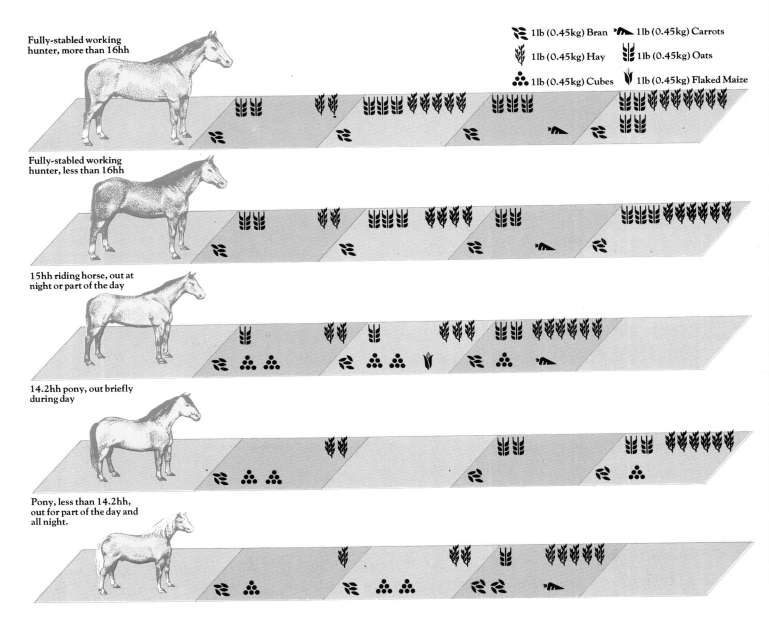

Fully-stabled working hunter, more than 16hh

Fully-stabled working hunter, less than 16hh

15hh riding horse, out at night or part of the day

14.2hh pony, out briefly during day

Pony, less than 14.2hh, out for part of the day and all night.

🌾 1lb (0.45kg) Bran ➤ 1lb (0.45kg) Carrots
🌾 1lb (0.45kg) Hay 🌾 1lb (0.45kg) Oats
⁘ 1lb (0.45kg) Cubes 🌾 1lb (0.45kg) Flaked Maize

weight of horse and the work it is expected to do; a hunter needs more exercise than a hack.

As with feeding, there are a few basic rules to remember. Most importantly, never exercise a horse until 1½ hours after a heavy feed; 1 hour after a small one. In any case, always remove the haynet an hour before exercise. Horses full of hay find breathing difficult when being worked hard.

The point of exercise is to get and keep the horse fit enough for the demands being made on it. A horse brought up from grass, say, is likely to be in 'grass condition'. In such a case, fitness can be achieved only through a rigidly controlled programme of exercise and feeding. Restrict exercise to walking, preferably on roads, for a week. Then combine walking with slow trotting. Soon, work can start in the school, while the period of road work can also be extended. Increase the

Above *The amount of food a horse requires varies according to its size, temperament and the type of work it will be doing. This chart gives basic specimen diets for horses with an even temperament. The amount and type of food given to each individual horse should be adapted according to observation.*

amount of grain fed in proportion to the extra in work. By the end of six weeks, the horse should be ready to be cantered over distances not exceeding 0.8km (½ mile). In the ninth week, it can have a gallop for up to 1.2km (¾ mile), but this should be strictly controlled so that the horse does not gallop flat out at full speed.

Indications of success are an increase in muscle and the disappearance of the profuse, lathery sweat of the out-of-condition horse. Never try to hurry the process; a horse cannot be conditioned through cantering and galloping, but only by slow, steady, regular work. This applies just as much to stabled horses

and ponies.

Always aim to end the exercise with a walk so that the horse comes back to its stable or field cool and relaxed. Once the tack has been removed, inspect the horse for cuts and bruises, pick out its feet, and brush off the saddle and sweat marks. Then rug up or groom. If you have been caught in the rain trot the horse home so that it is warm on arrival. Untack, and then give the horse a thorough rubbing down, either with straw or a towel. When this has been completed, cover the back with a layer of straw or use a sweat sheet. It is vital to keep the back warm to avoid the risk of colds and chills.

A thorough drying is essential if the horse is very hot and sweaty, but it will need to be sponged down first with lukewarm water. Either restrict sponging to the sweaty areas — usually the neck, chest and flanks — or sponge the entire body. Then, scrape off the surplus water with a sweat scraper, taking care to work with, and not against, the run of the coat. Next, rub down and, finally, cover with a sweat sheet. If possible, lead the horse around until it is completely dry.

Horses that have been worked exceptionally hard – in hunting, say, or in competitions – need further care. On returning to the stable, give the horse a drink of warm water. Then follow the procedures outlined above. Feed the horse with a bran mash and then leave it to rest. Return later to check that the animal is warm enough or has not broken out into a fresh sweat. Check for warmth by feeling the bases of the ears. If they are cold, warm by rubbing them with the hand and then put more blankets on the horse. If the latter, rub down again and walk the horse around until it is completely dry.

Grooming the horse

The chief point of grooming is to keep the horse clean, massage the skin and tone up the muscles. Field-kept horses need less grooming than stabled horses, particularly in winter, but some must nevertheless be carried out.

A good grooming kit is essential. This should consist of a dandy brush, to remove mud and dried sweat marks; a body brush, a soft, short-bristled brush for the head, body,

legs, mane and tail; a rubber curry comb, used to remove thickly-caked mud or matted hair, and a metal one, for cleaning the body brush; a water brush, used damp on the mane, tail and hooves; a hoof pick; a stable rubber, used to give a final polish to the coat; and some foam rubber sponges, for cleaning the eyes, nostrils, muzzle and dock.

Where more than one horse is kept, each animal should have its own grooming kit, kept together in a box or bag and clearly marked. This helps to prevent the risk of infection in cases of illness.

Grooming falls into three stages, each of which is carried out at a different time of the day. The first of these is quartering, normally done first thing in the morning before exercise. Tie up the horse. Then, pick the feet out and, next, clean the eyes, muzzle and dock with a damp sponge. If worn, rugs should be unbuckled and folded back and the head, neck, chest and forelegs cleaned with a body brush. Replace the rugs and repeat the process on the rear part of the body. Remove any stable stains with a water brush. Finish by brushing the mane and tail thoroughly with the body brush.

Strapping is the name given to the thorough grooming which follows exercise, when the horse has cooled down. Once again, tie the horse up and pick out its feet.

Follow by using the dandy brush to remove all traces of dirt, mud and sweat, paying particular attention to marks left by the girth and saddle and on the legs. Work from ears to tail, first on the near side and then on the off. Take care to use the brush lightly to avoid irritating the skin.

Next, comes the body brush. This must be used firmly for full effect. Start with the mane, pushing it to the wrong side to remove scurf from the roots. Brush the forelock. Then, start on the body, working from head to tail and grooming the nearside first, as before. Work with a circular motion, finishing in the direction of the hairs, and flick the brush outwards at the end of each stroke to push dust away from the body. At intervals, clean the brush with the curry comb, which is held in the other hand. It can be emptied by tapping on the floor at intervals.

Brush the head, remembering that this is one of the most sensitive areas of the horse. So use the brush firmly, but gently, and take particular care when grooming around the eyes, ears and nostrils. Finally, brush the tail – a few hairs at a time – so that every tangle is removed.

The next stage is wisping, which helps tone up the muscles and also stimulates the circulation. A wisp is a bundle of soft hay, twisted up to form a rope. Slightly dampen it,

Specimen exercise routine
based on a 16hh hunter

Exercise	Care and Management	Special Features	Exercise	Care and Management	Special Features
Week 1			**Week 5**		
20 mins walking on the first day, increasing gradually to one hour	Gradually increase food concentrate, begin strapping	During the pre-work week the horse's feet must be checked and shod. All horses require one rest day each working week	After first walking and trotting, the horse may have a short, slow canter on soft ground. Then decrease pace gradually	Four feeds a day – increase concentrates and reduce time at grass. Re-shoe if necessary	At this stage the coat should shine and the muscles should be hardening
Week 2			**Week 6**		
Walking for 1¼–1½ hrs over a 6–8 mile circuit	Check condition of legs and feet, watch for skin galls. Increase corn and vitamin supplements	Quiet lanes and roads with good surfaces are best for road work	A medium canter of reasonable length. Work at a sitting trot can now be started	Increase concentrate ration. Maintain thorough strapping	Schooling can be intensified by trotting in smaller circles, and work at the canter
Week 3			**Week 7**		
Always walk the first ½ mile. Then introduce very short spells of trotting, increasing their length gradually	Stable the horse at night and establish a regular routine	Schooling and lungeing in large circles can now be started	Canters can speed up. A short half speed gallop may be added at the end of the week (on good ground). Jumping can begin	The horse will sweat and should wear a rug at night	The final phase of building up to full work. It is useful to introduce the horse to travelling and to company at this stage
Week 4			**Week 8**		
1½–2 hrs work daily – split into schooling, lungeing and road work. More frequent, periods of trotting	Increase food concentrates	Trotting up gentle slopes can commence and increase slowly	On day 2 the horse can gallop at half speed up a gentle slope. Always walk the final mile	Full rations of concentrate. The horse should gallop on alternate days, and do steady work on the others. Renew shoes	When the horse is fully conditioned thorough exercise must be maintained on days when it does not work

Exercise needs always differ, according to the size of horse, the type of work it is doing and what it is being prepared for. Vary the routine accordingly

Left *The grooming kit. Ideally every horse should have its own to reduce the chance of any infection being passed from one to another. Keep the kit in a wire basket or bag so that no item is mislaid. Clean the equipment from time to time with a mild disinfectant. 1 Mane combs are used when mane or tail is plaited, trimmed or pulled. 2 Sponges, one for cleaning eyes, lips and nostrils, the second for cleaning the dock. 3 Can of hoof oil and brush, used to improve appearance of hoof and treat brittle feet. 4 Dandy brush (hard) to remove dried mud and sweat. 5 Body brush (soft) to remove dust and scurf. 6 Water brush (soft), for laying mane and tail and washing feet. 7 Sweat scraper, to remove water and sweat from coat. 8 Rubber curry comb, removes dirt from body brush; can also be used in place of dandy brush. 9 Metal curry comb, for cleaning dirt from body brush (never used on the horse). 10 Stable rubber used for final polishing of coat. 11 Hoof pick, for taking dirt and stones from the feet.*

and use vigorously on the neck, shoulders, quarters and thighs, concentrating on the muscular areas. Bang the wisp down hard on these, sliding it off with, not against, the coat. Take care to avoid bony areas and the tender region of the loins.

Sponge the eyes, lips, and muzzle and nostrils. Then, with a second sponge to minimize the risk of possible infection, wash round the dock and under the tail. Lift the tail as high as possible, so the entire region can be adequately cleaned. 'Lay' the mane with the water brush. Then brush the outside of the feet, taking care not to get water into the hollow of the heel. When the hooves are dry, brush hoof oil over the outside of each hoof as high as the coronet.

Finally, work over the horse with the stable rubber for a final polish. The object is to remove the last traces of dust from the coat. Fold the rubber into a flat bundle, dampen it slightly, and then go over the coat, working in the direction of the lay of the hair.

Strapping takes from between half to three-quarters of an hour with practice. It will normally take a novice slightly longer, largely because of the unaccustomed strain it imposes on the groom's muscles. 'Setting fair' – the last grooming of the day – takes far less time. Simply brush the horse lightly with the body brush, wisp and then put on the night rug (blanket), if one is normally worn.

Travelling with a horse

Careful planning when entering for a horse show, say, or going for a day's hunting, is essential if the horse is to arrive fit enough to undertake the tasks demanded of it. The first essential is to plan the journey; a fit horse can be hacked for up to ten miles, walking and trotting at an average speed of no more than six mph (a grass-kept pony's average should not be more than four mph). However, if the distance involved is greater than this, transport will be needed.

Horse boxes or car-towed trailers are the usual method of transport over long distances. Apart from the obvious mechanical checks that should be carried out before each journey, the horse's own requirements, too, need attention. A hay net is one essential; this should be filled with hay and given to the horse during the journey, unless the animal is expected to work hard immediately on arrival. Others include a first aid kit; rugs (day and sweat); bandages; grooming kit; a head collar; a water bucket and a filled water container. This last item is essential if the journey is to be a particularly long one, when the horse will need to be watered perhaps once or even twice en route.

In some cases – when hunting, for example

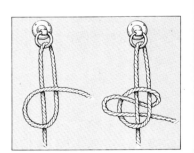

Above *How to tie a quick-release knot. This type of knot, which is easy to undo in an emergency, should always secure a horse. A quick tug on the free end releases the knot, but the more a horse pulls against it, the tighter it becomes.*

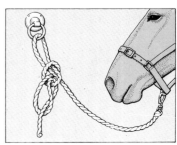

Intelligent ponies can learn by observation to pull at the free end of the quick-release knot and so get loose. If a pony learns to free itself in this way, it can usually be out-witted if the free end of the rope is passed back through the loop again (above).

To pick up a horse's foot, stand facing its tail. Warm it first by sliding a hand down from its shoulder to its fetlock. This can also encourage the horse to move its weight over to the other legs. It also helps to keep a young horse calm.

Working from the frog to the toe and concentrating on the edges first, use the point of the hoof pick to prise out any foreign objects lodged in the foot. Pebbles wedged between the frog and the bar can cause lameness. Take care not to push the point into the frog.

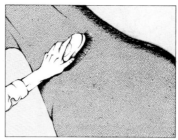

The dandy brush is used to remove heavy dirt caked mud and sweat stains, particularly from the saddle region, belly, points of hocks, fetlocks and pasterns. As it is fairly harsh it should not be used on the more tender areas, or on a recently clipped horse.

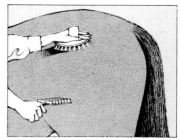

A body brush has short, dense bristles designed to penetrate and clean the coat. It should be applied with some pressure, in firm, circular movements. After a few strokes clear it of dust with a curry comb. A gentler brushing should be given round the head.

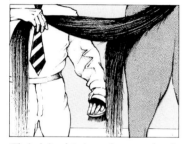

The body brush is also used to groom the tail. This should be brushed a few hairs at a time, starting with the undermost ones. Remove all mud and tangles, taking care not to break any hairs. Finally, the whole tail should be brushed into shape from the top.

Wring out a soft sponge in warm water and sponge the eyes first, wiping outwards from the corners. Carefully sponge round eyelids. Wring out the sponge and wipe over the muzzle, lips and nostrils. A separate sponge should be used to sponge the dock area.

The water brush is used to 'lay' the mane. The tip of the brush is dipped in a bucket of water and thoroughly shaken before it is applied. Keeping the brush flat, make firm, downward strokes from the roots. The mane should be left neat and slightly damp.

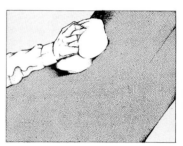

As a final touch to the grooming go over the whole coat with the stable-rubber to remove any trace of dust. This cloth is used slightly damp and folded into a flat bundle. Work along the lie of the hair. The stable-rubber leaves the coat gleaming.

– the horse can travel saddled-up, with a rug placed over the saddle, but, in the case of competitions, a rug alone should be worn. Travelling bandages should always be used, as well as a tail bandage to stop the top of the tail from being rubbed. In addition, knee caps and hock boots should be worn as an added protection.

Preparation of the horse itself must start the night before, with an especially thorough grooming. Both mane and tail should be washed. A grass-kept horse should be kept in for the night, if possible. The next morning, follow the normal stable routine, with the addition of a drawn-out strapping. Remember that, in the case of a show, the mane should be plaited; this can be started the night before to ease the task of getting the mane into shape, but will need to be completed the following day.

Loading the horse

Getting a horse into a box or trailer is an easy enough task, provided that the process is tackled calmly and without undue haste. The simplest way is for one person to lead the horse forward, walking straight forward and resisting the temptation to pull at the head. A couple of helpers should stand behind the horse in case help is required, but out of kicking range.

The main reason for a horse showing reluctance to enter a box is usually its fear of the noise of its hooves on the ramp. This can be overcome by putting down some straw to deaden the sound. Loading another, calmer, horse first, or tempting a horse forward with a feed bucket containing a handful of oats, also act as encouragements.

A really obstinate horse, however, will have to be physically helped into the box. The way to do this is to attach two ropes to the ramp's rails, so that they cross just above the horse's hocks, with two helpers in position – one at each end of the ropes. As the horse approaches the ramp, they tighten the ropes to propel the animal into the box.

Tack – care and maintenance

Care of saddles and bridles is just as important as care of the horse itself. Ill-fitting, dirty or worn tack is not only unpleasant and uncomfortable for the horse; it can also be extremely dangerous for the rider. Therefore always keep tack clean and check it regularly for wear. With saddles this applies particularly to girths and stirrup leathers – a badly-worn girth is a potential killer. Bits should never be allowed to become worn and rough.

All tack should be stored in a cool, dry place – a purpose-planned tack room is the best. A warm, damp atmosphere will cause

Above A half-completed wisp. The wisp is used after body brushing, when strapping a horse. It should be rubbed vigorously over the muscular areas, avoiding the head and sensitive parts. Wisping stimulates circulation, gives a form of massage and shines the coat. The wisp is used damp and brought down with a bang in the direction of the lay of the coat.

A wisp is made from soft hay, dampened slightly and then twisted round a core of twine to form a rope about 2m (7ft) long. This is formed into a firm, fist-sized pad by making two loops and weaving the rest of the rope through them as shown above in loose form. A properly made wisp should be hard and firm and no larger than can conveniently be grasped in the hand.

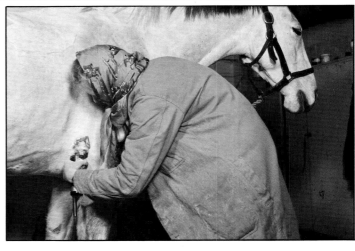

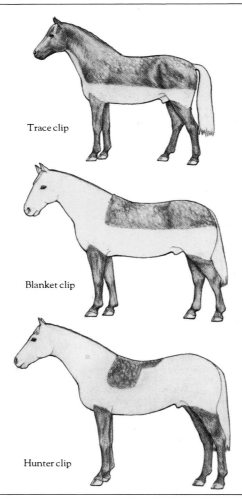

Trace clip

Blanket clip

Hunter clip

*Clipping is done chiefly for comfort, as the thicker winter coat grown during the autumn can lead to heavy sweating during exercise. Removing all, or part, of it prevents this, lessens the chance of a horse getting chilled and makes it easier to groom. The trace clip (**top right**) is the minimum clip, removing hair only from the chest, belly, upper legs, elbows and up the back of the quarters. It keeps the protective warmth of the coat, while preventing heavy sweating. The blanket clip (**centre**) is slightly cooler, leaving a blanket-shaped area of body hair and all the leg hair on for warmth. In the hunter clip (**bottom**) all the coat is clipped, leaving only the leg hair as protection from thorns and scratches. Sometimes a saddle patch is left. This prevents the saddle rubbing and increases the comfort of horse and rider.*

Pulling a mane or tail is done mainly for smartness. Pulling a mane thins it, makes it lie flat and evens the edge. Tail pulling slims the tail by removing short hairs from the top. Grass-kept horses, however, need the protection of a natural, thick tail to keep themselves free from flies, which can be very troublesome in the summer.

Above *Clipping the horse is a lengthy and delicate operation, care should be taken not to upset the animal. The coat should first be dry and well-groomed.*

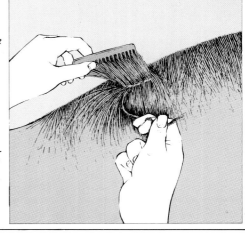

Right *Pulling the mane. Remove the longer underhairs, starting from the withers and working towards the head. It is best done when the horse is warm after exercise. Lift the top hairs clear with a comb, then wind a few strands around the fingers – and pluck them out.*

leather to crack, break or develop mould. Similarly, metal parts will tarnish or rust. Always hang bridles up on a bridle rack; saddles should be placed over a saddle horse, or on a wide padded bracket screwed firmly to the wall.

Tack should be cleaned daily; at the very least, sweat marks should be removed and the bit thoroughly cleaned. The equipment needed is as follows: a rough towel or large sponge for washing; a small, flat sponge; a chamois leather; saddle soap; metal polish or wool; a couple of soft cloths; a dandy brush; a nail, to clean curb hooks; a bucket; hanging hooks for bridle, girths and leathers; a saddle horse; and a vegetable oil.

When cleaning the saddle, place it on the saddle horse and remove all fittings, such as girths and stirrup leathers. These should be cleaned separately. Wash the leatherwork with lukewarm water to remove dirt, dried sweat and grease – but take care not to get the saddle saturated. If the lining is of leather, it can also be washed. Otherwise scrub it down dry with a dandy brush.

With the chamois leather slightly dam-

pened, dry the saddle off. Apply saddle soap liberally with the damp sponge, working it well into the saddle to get the soap into the leather without creating a lather. Allow some time for the leather to absorb the soap. Then rub over with a moist sponge and, finally, wipe down with the chamois leather. Clean the leather pieces that have been removed with saddle soap, and the metal ones with metal polish. Clean out the holes of stirrup leathers with a match or a nail. Leather girths should be oiled on the inside. Web string and nylon ones should be brushed down with a dandy brush and washed occasionally, using pure soap. Then, reassemble.

As a preliminary to cleaning, it is a good idea to take the bridle to pieces so that the stitching can be thoroughly checked for wear. Reassemble, and, starting with the bit, wash with lukewarm water. Dry, soap the leather and polish the metal in the same way as the saddle. If the leather needs oiling, take the bridle apart once cleaning has been completed. Oil each piece individually. Then fit the parts together again, taking care that the bit is in the correct position.

Bridles and bits

All commonly-used bridles have the same purpose – to hold the bit in the mouth. It is through use of this, in conjunction with seat and legs, that the horse is guided and controlled. There are two main types of bridle – the snaffle bridle, with one bit, and the double bridle, with two. The latter has two bits and two sets of reins.

All modern bits are based on one of two principles – either the snaffle or the curb. The snaffle is a mild bit. It consists of a metal bar, either jointed or plain, with a ring at either end to which the rein and headpiece of the bridle are attached. Pressure on the bit via the rein causes it to act on the corners of the horse's mouth, with a nutcracker action if the bit is jointed.

The curb is also of metal; it may have a hump, called a port, in the middle. It is fitted with shanks at either end, the cheekpieces being attached to the top of the shanks and the rein to rings at the bottom. The shanks are linked by a chain which lies in the chin groove.

Pressure on the rein has a leverage effect –

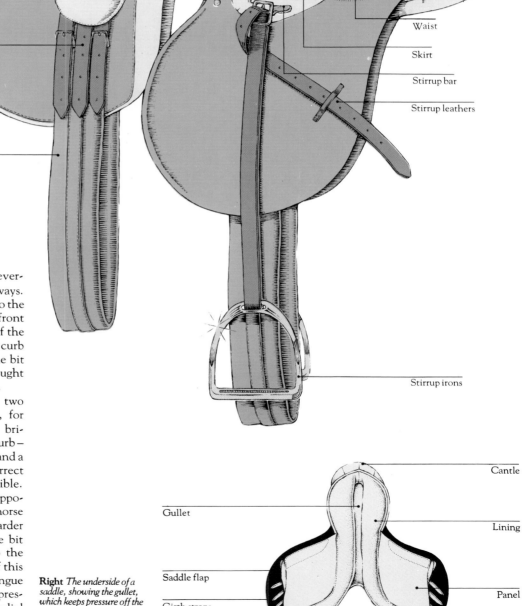

Right *A general-purpose saddle, showing its parts. A well-fitting saddle must distribute the rider's weight evenly, without undue pressure on the withers and loins. It should not restrict a horse's shoulder movements, and must suit the build of the rider.*

Saddle flap

Point pocket (for point of tree)

Buckle guard

Girth straps

Girth

Cantle

Lining (part of panel)

Pommel

Seat

Waist

Skirt

Stirrup bar

Stirrup leathers

Stirrup irons

the longer the shanks, the greater the leverage. This causes the bit to act in three ways. The mouthpiece presses downwards on to the bars of the mouth (the gap between the front incisors and the back molars), the top of the headpiece presses on to the poll, and the curb chain tightens in the chin groove. If the bit has a high port, the top of it will be brought into contact with the roof of the mouth.

There are many variations of these two basic types of bit. The double bridle, for example, uses a jointed snaffle bit (a bridoon) in combination with an English curb – a curb fitted with short, straight shanks and a lip-strap to keep the curb chain in the correct position. Always use the mildest bit possible. A severe bit often produces exactly the opposite result to the one intended, as the horse can easily become upset, excitable and harder to control. Above all, avoid using the bit insensitively, as this will only lead to the horse developing a hard mouth. Signs of this are the corners of the mouth and the tongue becoming calloused through constant pressure from the bit. If this happens, remedial action should be taken immediatley.

Right *The underside of a saddle, showing the gullet, which keeps pressure off the horse's spine, even when the rider is in the saddle.*

Gullet

Saddle flap

Girth straps

Cantle

Lining

Panel

Selecting a saddle

As with bridles and bits, there are various types of saddle – some designed for a particular task, or, as in the case of the Western saddle, a specific style of riding. The most important thing to remember is that the saddle must fit the horse properly. An ill-fitting saddle will make the horse and rider very sore; and it will also make it impossible for the rider to position himself correctly.

The framework of the saddle is called the tree and determines the final shape, so it must be correctly made. Many riding associations, such as the Pony Club, have their own approved patterns and it is always safest to look for one of these. The commonest form in use today is the 'spring tree' – so-called because it has two pieces of light steel let into it under the seat to increase resilience. Treat the tree with care. If a saddle is dropped the tree may break. The saddle cannot then be used until it is professionally repaired.

The rest of the saddle consists of layers of webbing, canvas, serge, and finally, leather. The padded part, which rests on the horse's back, is usually made of felt or stuffed with wool. It is important that this padding is arranged so that the rider's weight is distributed evenly over the back and carried on the fleshy part rather than the spine. This helps to preserve the horse's strength and stamina and prevents sores from developing. If additional protection is necessary, a pad – known as a numnah – can be placed beneath the saddle.

Girths keep the saddle in place, so they must be strong. They should be inspected

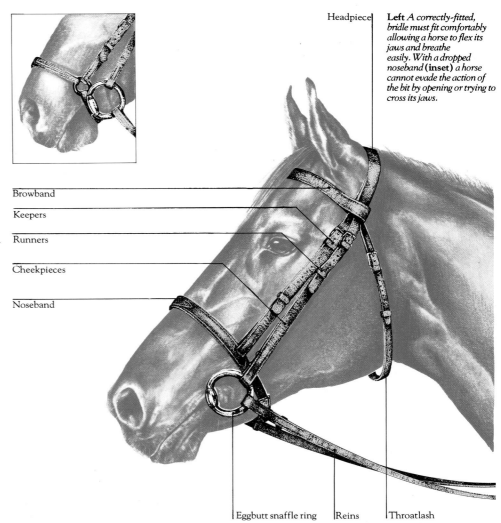

Headpiece

Browband

Keepers

Runners

Cheekpieces

Noseband

Eggbutt snaffle ring | Reins | Throatlash

Left A correctly-fitted, bridle must fit comfortably allowing a horse to flex its jaws and breathe easily. With a dropped noseband (inset) a horse cannot evade the action of the bit by opening or trying to cross its jaws.

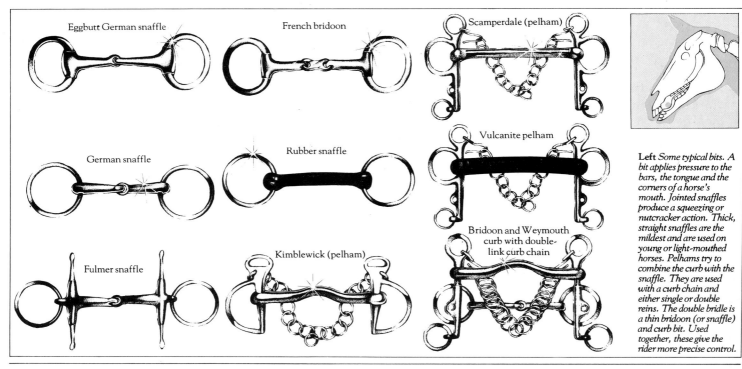

Eggbutt German snaffle

French bridoon

Scamperdale (pelham)

German snaffle

Rubber snaffle

Vulcanite pelham

Fulmer snaffle

Kimblewick (pelham)

Bridoon and Weymouth curb with double-link curb chain

Left Some typical bits. A bit applies pressure to the bars, the tongue and the corners of a horse's mouth. Jointed snaffles produce a squeezing or nutcracker action. Thick, straight snaffles are the mildest and are used on young or light-mouthed horses. Pelhams try to combine the curb with the snaffle. They are used with a curb chain and either single or double reins. The double bridle is a thin bridoon (or snaffle) and curb bit. Used together, these give the rider more precise control.

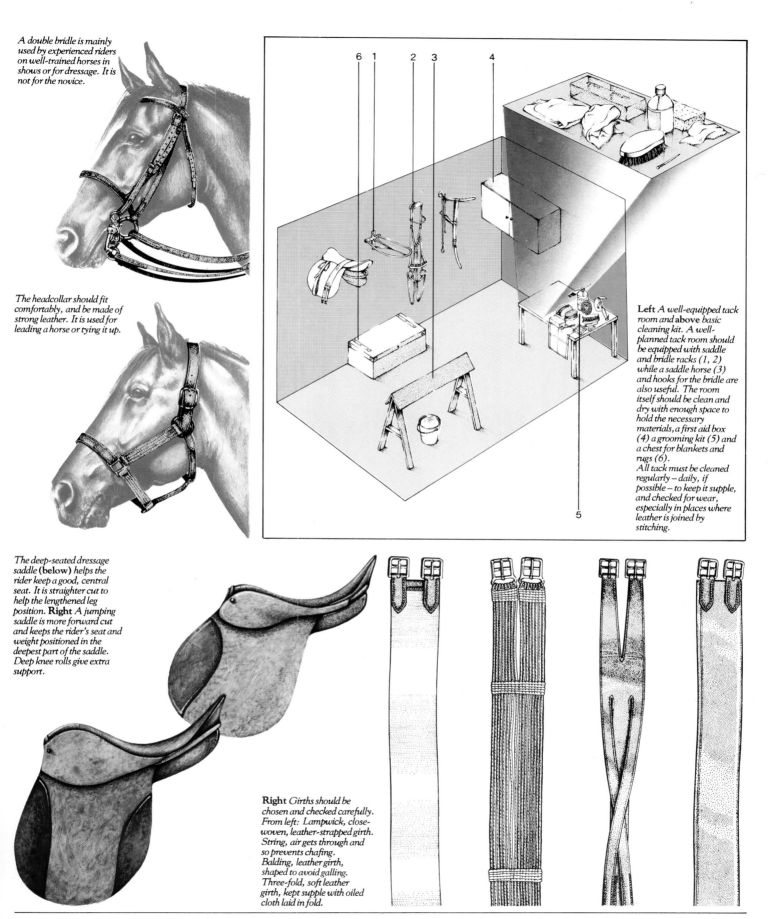

A double bridle is mainly used by experienced riders on well-trained horses in shows or for dressage. It is not for the novice.

The headcollar should fit comfortably, and be made of strong leather. It is used for leading a horse or tying it up.

Left *A well-equipped tack room and* **above** *basic cleaning kit. A well-planned tack room should be equipped with saddle and bridle racks (1, 2) while a saddle horse (3) and hooks for the bridle are also useful. The room itself should be clean and dry with enough space to hold the necessary materials, a first aid box (4) a grooming kit (5) and a chest for blankets and rugs (6).*
All tack must be cleaned regularly – daily, if possible – to keep it supple, and checked for wear, especially in places where leather is joined by stitching.

The deep-seated dressage saddle **(below)** *helps the rider keep a good, central seat. It is straighter cut to help the lengthened leg position.* **Right** *A jumping saddle is more forward cut and keeps the rider's seat and weight positioned in the deepest part of the saddle. Deep knee rolls give extra support.*

Right *Girths should be chosen and checked carefully. From left: Lampwick, close-woven, leather-strapped girth. String, air gets through and so prevents chafing. Balding, leather girth, shaped to avoid galling. Three-fold, soft leather girth, kept supple with oiled cloth laid in fold.*

Top *New Zealand rug, an outdoor rug of waterproof canvas partly lined with wool, with straps* (inset) *to keep it in place.* Left centre, *woollen day rug, bound with braid, worn for warmth in stable during day or for travelling.* Right centre, *sweat sheet, open cotton mesh, used to cool an overheated horse, or under a night rug if horse sweats.* Below right *Wool-lined night rug, of hemp or jute, for warmth at night in stable.* Below left *Woollen blankets worn under day or night rugs for extra warmth are put well forward on neck and clear of tail. Any surplus is folded back over rug.*

regularly for wear. They can be made of leather, webbing, or nylon string – in the case of webbing, two girths should be used for additional safety. Stirrup irons, too, should always be chosen with safety foremost in mind. Safety irons, often used by children, are specifically designed so that the foot will come free in a fall. Adults should always check that there is 12mm (½in) clearance on either side of the foot, measured at the widest place of the boot or shoe, so that it does not become jammed.

Horse clothing

Many different types of clothing have been developed to keep the horse warm, protect it from injury, or give its limbs added support. Chief amongst these are rugs and bandages.

Rugs are especially useful as protection after a horse has been clipped, but special types are used for other purposes as well. In all cases, it is vital that the blanket should fit properly and be securely fastened. A roller must be used to keep a night rug in place.

Bandages fall into three categories. Tail bandages are used to make the top of the tail look neat and to protect it during a journey. Stable bandages, covering the area from the knee right down is underneath the fetlock, keep the legs warm, and, similarly, are used as protection during travelling. Exercise bandages, support the back tendons and protect the legs from thorns.

Clipping

Horses are clipped to maintain comfort and, less importantly, for smartness. Removing all

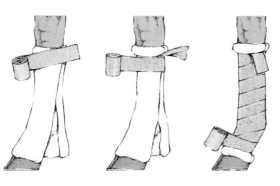

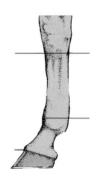

Right *Four stages in fitting a stable bandage. Pad beneath all bandages with cotton wool or an equivalent. Wool stable bandages are rolled evenly down from below the knee or hock to the coronet, then upwards to the start and tied on side of leg.* **Far right** *Placing of crêpe exercise or pressure bandage to support back tendons and protect the leg. These bandages are applied firmly and often stitched in place for greater security.*

or part of the coat by clipping prevents heavy sweating during exercise in winter and therefore lessens the risk of a horse catching a chill. It also enables the horse to dry off more quickly.

There are various types of clip; choice should depend on what the horse is expected to do, and how much it sweats doing it. Remember that a clipped horse will need to wear rugs for warmth during cold weather, if it is kept in either a stable or a field.

Health and the horse

Horses are tough creatures, but, like any animal, they can fall ill or be injured. A healthy pony or horse is alert, bright eyed, and takes a keen interest in all that goes on around it. Ribs and hip bones should not be prominent, and the quarters should be well-rounded. The animal should stand square on all four legs. The base of the ears should be warm to the touch.

Signs of illness vary, but there are some general symptoms which can give warning of trouble to come. A field-kept pony which stays for a long time in one place, a horse which goes off its food, a willing horse which suddenly becomes 'nappy' – all these signs are indications that something is wrong. Other symptoms include: discharge from the eyes or nostrils; stumbling for no apparent reason; restlessness; dullness of eye or general lack of interest; sweating; kicking or biting at the flank; lameness; diarrhoea; persistent rubbing of the neck or quarters against a wall or fence; apparent difficulty in breathing; coughing.

It is essential, therefore, to have a reliable vet, and, if ever in any doubt, to call him without hesitation. Better to pay for a visit than to run the risk of mistaken self-diagnosis leading to a more serious illness, or even death. Nevertheless, all horse owners should have a practical knowledge of first aid, and a first aid kit is an essential part of any stable.

*Brushing boots of felt or leather, and rubber over-reach boots, are often worn for protection in training and eventing, or when a horse moves too closely in front (**top left**), so knocking one leg with the other, or hits the heel of its forefoot with toe of hind foot (**top right**).*

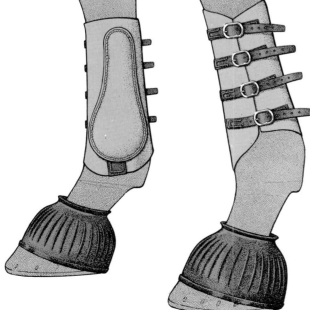

Fitting a stockinette tail bandage. Dampen hair with water brush. Unroll short length of dry bandage and place this beneath tail, close to dock.

Holding the end of the bandage against the tail, make one turn to secure the bandage. Then continue the bandaging evenly downwards.

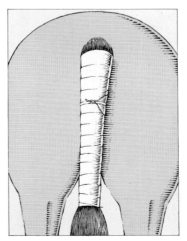
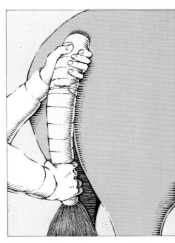

The tail bandage should stop just short of the last tail bone and the remaining length should be bandaged upwards and secured with tapes.

Finally bend the tail into a comfortable position. Tail bandages should not be left overnight. Slide them off, downwards, with both hands.

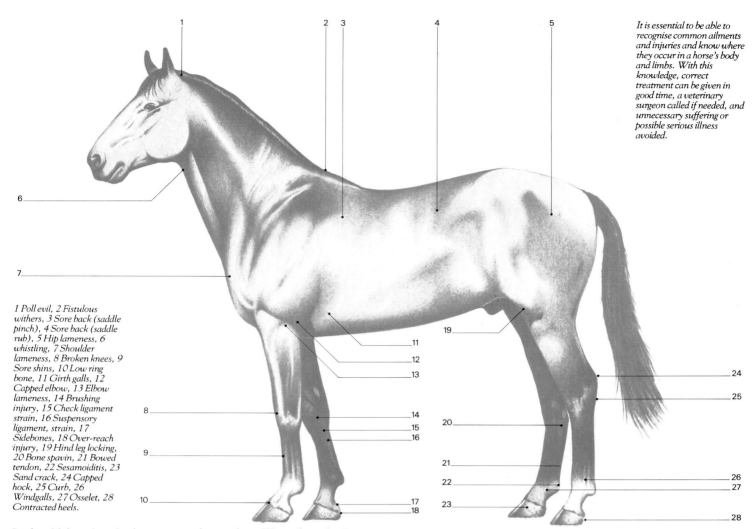

It is essential to be able to recognise common ailments and injuries and know where they occur in a horse's body and limbs. With this knowledge, correct treatment can be given in good time, a veterinary surgeon called if needed, and unnecessary suffering or possible serious illness avoided.

1 Poll evil, 2 Fistulous withers, 3 Sore back (saddle pinch), 4 Sore back (saddle rub), 5 Hip lameness, 6 whistling, 7 Shoulder lameness, 8 Broken knees, 9 Sore shins, 10 Low ring bone, 11 Girth galls, 12 Capped elbow, 13 Elbow lameness, 14 Brushing injury, 15 Check ligament strain, 16 Suspensory ligament, strain, 17 Sidebones, 18 Over-reach injury, 19 Hind leg locking, 20 Bone spavin, 21 Bowed tendon, 22 Sesamoiditis, 23 Sand crack, 24 Capped hock, 25 Curb, 26 Windgalls, 27 Osselet, 28 Contracted heels.

It should be placed where it can be easily found in an emergency.

Lameness

Lameness is the commonest form of disability in the horse. Treating most forms of it is usually best left to an expert.

To find the source of the lameness, first establish which leg is causing the pain. Do this by having the horse led at a slow trot – downhill, if possible. If one of the forelegs is lame, the horse will nod its head as the other leg touches the ground. Similarly, if the hind legs are involved, the horse's weight will fall on the sound leg. Next, feel for heat, pain and swelling. Start with the foot, as 90 per cent of all lameness is centred there.

Causes of lameness can range from a simple stone in the foot to actual disease. Consult the chart for details and possible treatment. The most serious disease is laminitis (founder), when prompt veterinary attention is essential to avoid the risk of permanent injury to the horse. This is one of the most painful conditions from which the horse can suffer.

Wounds and other injuries

Wounds and injuries are another common problem. Puncture cuts, caused by thorns, say, can easily occur during exercise. This is one of the reasons why exercise bandages should always be worn. Always call the vet if the wound looks deep, or if you think stitching is required.

First bring the bleeding under control. Small cuts should cease bleeding on their own within 20 minutes, but, if the cut is serious or bleeding does not stop, apply a pressure bandage. Clip the hair from the skin around the wound and clean it thoroughly. Gently trickle cold water over it from a hose pipe, or wash the area with saline solution. Then coat with an anti-biotic powder and dress, if possible. Do not bandage too tightly; a tight bandage will cause pain if swelling occurs. Keep the wound clean and check.

The most serious of all infections is tetanus, caused by bacteria in the soil penetrating the skin through the wound. All horses should be immunized against the disease by an initial course of injections, followed by regular 'boosters'. If in any doubt, it is best to

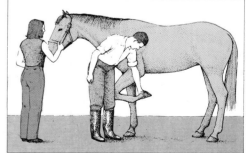

Above Lifting a front foot helps keep the horse still during examination.

Below Kicking is unlikely, when handling hind legs, if tail is held firmly down.

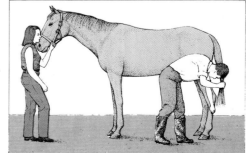

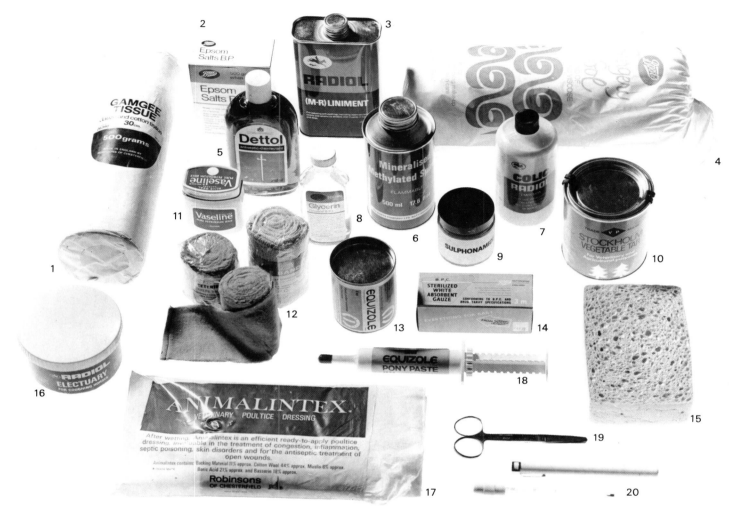

Every stable should have a medicine chest stocked with a first aid kit and medicines for everyday ailments. It should be conveniently

placed and kept clean and tidy. Clear identification of the kit and contents is essential. **Above** *A typical basic kit containing:*

1 Gamgee tissue, 2 Epsom salts, 3 Liniment, 4 Roll of cotton wool, 5 Antiseptic, 6 Methylated spirit, 7 Specific for colic, 8 Glycerine, 9

Sulphonamide powder, 10 Stockholm tar, 11 Petroleum jelly, 12 Assorted bandages, 13 Worming remedy, 14 Sterilized gauze,

15 Sponge, 16 Coughing electuary, 17 Ready-to-apply poultice, 18 Worm paste in dispenser, 19 Round-ended surgical

scissors, 20 Thermometer. Substitutions can be made to this selection. Opinions vary as to the amount of equipment needed.

have the horse immunized again. The injections cannot kill – tetanus will, unless treatment is administered speedily.

Other injuries are normally the result of falls, kicks, or irritations – the latter frequently the result of ill-fitting tack. Mouth injuries should be treated with salt water washes. Do not use a bit until the mouth has healed and check that this was not the initial cause of the injury. Girth galls and saddle sores should both be treated with fomentations. After they have healed, harden the affected areas with salt water or methylated spirit. Do not ride the horse with a saddle until the sore has completely healed.

Broken or cut knees can happen as the result of a fall. If the injury is more than skin deep, the vet should be called. Otherwise treat with cold water, as with a cut, and then

apply a soothing poultice. Carefully tie a figure of eight bandage.

Capped knees and hocks are usually the result of kicks or a blow. Treat the first with a rest, massage and a pressure bandage. The treatment for the second is cold water, and then a poultice. If any swelling persists, blister the area of the injury mildly.

Skin diseases

Like humans, horses can easily catch skin diseases, particularly in unhygienic conditions. Lice, for example, are a constant pest to a long-coated, field-kept horse, particularly in February. Other skin diseases include ringworm; sweet itch; mud fever; cracked heels; pustular dermititis (acne); warbles; and nettle rash. For their treatment, see the chart. Many of these diseases are highly con-

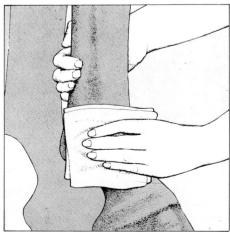

Above *Direct pressure is applied to stop persistent bleeding from a vein. A*

folded handkerchief should always be carried, as this can serve as a pad.

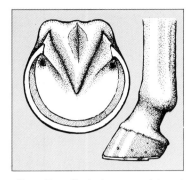

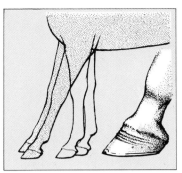

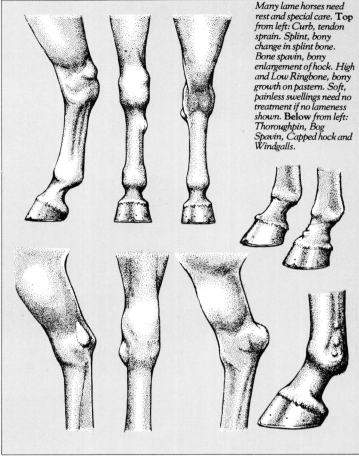

Many lame horses need rest and special care. **Top** from left: Curb, tendon sprain. Splint, bony change in splint bone. Bone spavin, bony enlargement of hock. High and Low Ringbone, bony growth on pastern. Soft, painless swellings need no treatment if no lameness shown. **Below** from left: Thoroughpin, Bog Spavin, Capped hock and Windgalls.

Above Corns (bruises) occur on sole in angle of wall and bar. After treatment, seated shoes (**inset**) relieve pressure.

Above Laminitis, inflammation of inner hoof wall, causes this stance. It can lead to ridging on hoof (**inset**).

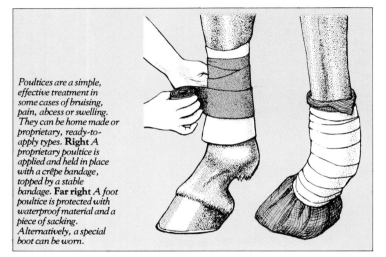

Poultices are a simple, effective treatment in some cases of bruising, pain, abcess or swelling. They can be home made or proprietary, ready-to-apply types. **Right** A proprietary poultice is applied and held in place with a crêpe bandage, topped by a stable bandage. **Far right** A foot poultice is protected with waterproof material and a piece of sacking. Alternatively, a special boot can be worn.

tagious — ringworm, for instance, can be transmitted to humans, as well as horses, in certain cases. Therefore, always observe strict sanitary precautions in the stable.

Chills, coughs and chest diseases
Refusing food, discharge from nostrils and eyes, listlessness, coughing and high temperature are all indications of a chill. Keep the horse warm and consult the vet, who will probably prescribe antibiotics in severe cases.

Coughs, too, should always be treated by the vet if they are persistent. Causes can vary from simple irritation, the result of feeding with dusty hay, to severe diseases, such as

epidemic cough and strangles. Other respiratory diseases include equine influenza; whistling; roaring; high blowing; and broken wind. For details, consult the chart.

If the horse is coughing, never work it hard. Rest and warmth are most important. Galloping a horse with a cough can, in extreme cases, lead to broken wind, which is incurable.

Digestive problems
Teeth and stomach can both give the horse problems. Both demand prompt attention if anything does go wrong.

Uneven wear on the teeth can lead to

sharp edges developing. These make chewing food painful; in addition, the mouth and cheeks may get cut. The remedy is to have the teeth filed (rasped). This must be done by an expert.

Restlessness, sweating, biting and kicking at the flank, lying down and getting up again are all signs of colic — acute pain in the abdomen. Colic falls into three types. These are spasmodic colic, so-called because the pain comes in spasms; flatulent colic, caused by a gas build-up because of a blockage in the bowel; and twisted gut, where the bowel itself, or the membrane supporting it, becomes twisted, so cutting off the blood

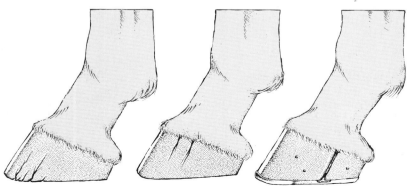

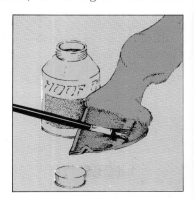

Hoofs of unshod horses at grass can become cracked if they are neglected. Grass cracks (**far left**) split up from base of wall. They grow out if the hoof is treated appropriately by the farrier. Sand cracks (**centre left**) split down from the hoof head. These are much more serious and need veterinary care. After treatment, they can be controlled with seated shoes (**left**), which take the pressure off the crack. Hoof cream and hoof oil (**right**) applied daily, help prevent cracks by keeping hoof healthy.

Strangles

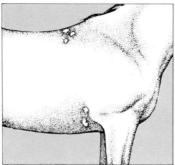
Saddle sores and girth galls

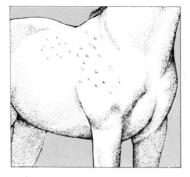
Ringworm

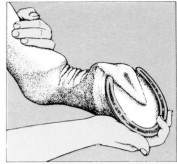
Cracked heels

Head

Symptoms:	Causes:	Treatment:	Symptoms:	Causes:	Treatment:
Blocked tear duct			**Colds and Coughs**		
Tears running down face	Sand, grit or mucous causing blockage of tear ducts	Call vet, who will probably clear blockage by using a catheter to force sterile liquid through the duct	Thin discharge from nostrils; coughing	Infection; sometimes dusty hay or allergy	Isolate animal and keep warm; give regular doses of cough medicine. Consult vet
Broken wind			**Influenza**		
Persistent cough, rapid exhaustion, double movement of flank	Breakdown of air vessels in the lung from overworking the horse	Incurable, may be alleviated by keeping horse out, work gently and dampen food	Lethargy, cough, high temperature. Horse refuses food	Virus infection	Isolate. Keep warm. Rest. Call vet. Prevention by inoculation is possible
Catarrh			**Strangles**		
Thick yellowish discharge from the nostrils	Inflammation of mucous membrane May be cold infection preceding cough or allergy, beware of infecting other horses	Clean nostrils with warm boracic solution and smear with petroleum jelly In summer, turn out to grass	Similar to those of influenza, plus swelling of lymph glands under the jaw, which eventually form abscesses	Contact with infected animal or with contaminated grooming kit, feed buckets, etc	Isolate. Call vet. Feed hay and bran mashes and keep horse warm. Rest is essential

supply and causing severe pain.

All forms of colic are exceptionally painful, as the horse is incapable of vomiting to obtain relief

Colic must be treated quickly, as real suffering is being caused. As long as the horse is not completely exhausted, lead it around gently and, if at all possible, prevent it from lying down. If the animal lies down and rolls, it may well injure itself. Keep the horse warm and the box or stall well bedded.

Treatment varies according to the type of colic involved, but, if no improvement occurs after an hour or if the pain is obviously severe, call a vet immediately. For spasms, give a colic drink (one should be kept ready made-up in the first aid kit) and for wind administer a laxative to open the bowels. A half to a pint of linseed oil, depending on the size of the horse involved, is a standard re-

medy. Linseed oil, too, is good in cases of constipation.

Constipation and diarrhoea present fewer problems, but worms – parasites present in all horses – can be a menace if not strictly controlled. They present particular problems to the owners of field-kept horses; here, prevention is better than cure . All horses, however, should be regularly wormed, by treating with a deworming medicine, as part of stable routing. Consult the vet as to the best dosage.

Azoturia is not strictly a digestive disease, but it is closely connected with correct feeding. It can occur when a horse is worked hard after being rested on a full working diet, though the exact cause of the disease is unknown. The first signs are slackening of pace and stiffness of muscles, particularly in the quarters. If the horse is urged on it will

eventually stagger, come to a halt and may even collapse. Always arrange for it to be transported back to the stable – never try to ride home. The vet must be called.

Treatment is rest, warmth, massage, plenty of water and a laxative diet. However, once infected, it is likely that the disease will reoccur. Therefore, always reduce the feed according to the amount of work actually being done by the horse.

Nursing the horse
Like all animals, horses take time to recover form illness. The vet will always instruct the owner in what to do, but, largely, successful nursing is merely a matter of common sense.

Giving medicine, for example, can present problems. The simplest way is in the feed, provided that the medicine is suitable and the horse is eating. Soluble medicines can be

Digestive system

Symptoms:	Causes:	Treatment:	Symptoms:	Causes:	Treatment:
Colic			**Diarrhoea**		
Severe abdominal pain, characterised by pawing of the ground, restlessness, sweating, rolling, lying down and getting up, kicking, biting and looking at the stomach, groaning, cold ears	Poor or irregular feeding, wrong sort of food, exercise or drinking straight after food, too much food when horse is tired. Worm infection	Call vet immediately. meanwhile do what you can to relieve the pain. Keep horse warm, apply hot water bottle to belly. Try to discourage horse from lying down or rolling	Very loose, watery droppings	Excessive fresh grass. Worms	Mix dry bran with food or add kaolin. Feed with hay. If persistant, call vet
			Worms		
			Loss of condition, in spite of careful feeding	There are several types of intestinal parasites collectively known as worms	Regular doses of worming powder or paste, coupled with regular maintenance of pasture

Skin and coat

Symptoms:	Causes:	Treatment:	Symptoms:	Causes:	Treatment:
Heat bumps (Humor)			**Sweet itch**		
Various forms of size and shape. Rarely seen all over horse	Probably overheating from too much protein in system	Give bran mash with addition of two tablespoons of Epsom salts.	Extreme itchiness of areas around mane and tail, apparent only in late spring, summer and early autumn	Unknown, probably an allergy	Apply calamine lotion to relieve itching. Keep mane and tail clean. Lard and sulphur applied to the area can be soothing. Consult vet
Lice			**Warbles**		
Itching, dull coat, appearance of small grey or black parasites on the coat	Unknown. Appears in spring on grass-fed horses or on animals which have been in poor condition and are now improving	Dust affected areas liberally with delousing powder, obtainable from vet. Keep grooming kit separate	Maggot of the warble fly	Painful swelling on back	Bathe in warm water which will keep the lump soft and help to 'draw' the warble from a small hole on the top of the swelling. The maggot can be gently squeezed out, but do not do this before consulting the vet
Ringworm					
Usually circular bare patches on the skin of varying sizes which may or may not be itchy	Fungus infection which is highly contagious	Apply tincture of iodine to affected parts. Disinfect rugs and sterilise grooming kit. Keep horse isolated			

Left A healthy horse is alert and attentive, taking a keen interest in its surroundings. It carries its head high, ears pricked, eyes bright and wide open. Its coat is smooth and glossy.

mixed in with the drinking water. Otherwise the vet will advise.

The golden rules of nursing are gentleness, cleanliness, and the ability to ensure the horse's comfort and rest. When treating a wound always try to keep the dust down in the stable. Reduce concentrated foods for a horse suddenly thrown out of work by lameness and substitute a mild laxative instead. Gentle sponging of eyes and nostrils will help refresh a horse with a raised temperature.

Care when old
Horses and ponies are frequently remarkably long lived. Some ponies, for instance, are still leading useful lives at thirty, but caring for an elderly horse presents its own set of problems.

Teeth must be regularly filed (rasped), as the molars will probably become long and sharp if left untreated. Select the diet carefully; boiled barley, broad bran, chaff and good quality hay form the best mixture for an old horse.

Eventually though, some horses just lose interest in life. If the lustre goes out of the eyes or the appetite wanes for no apparent reason, it is then kinder to have the horse put down. A vet will arrange this. A humane killer is used, and death is instantaneous.

Lack of work and boredom can cause severe stable vices like crib-biting (below) and weaving (right).